You're Crazy If You Don't Talk To Yourself

D1310822

By Steve Backlund

Dedicated to:
Mark and Maryann Perdue
For your amazing support

The Mountain Chapel Church Family
For encouraging me to go after my dreams

Craig and Cyndi Barber
For running with the vision in the Nevada desert

Sue Scott
For your encouragement and loyalty

Acknowledgements

Editing: Wendy Backlund, Kim Jaramillo, Leslie Taylor, Lorraine West

Special Assistance: Maureen Puddle

Front and Back Cover Design: Linda Lee

ISBN: 978-0-615-20970-8

TABLE OF CONTENTS

About The Author

Steve Backlund is known for his wisdom and practical insights on "how to do life." The students in our ministry school – Bethel School of Supernatural Ministry – love him because he always leaves them encouraged and refreshed in their vision. He has an unusual gift to take the mundane and make it exciting, and to take the familiar and make it new. **Bill Johnson, Bethel Church,** Redding, CA - Author of <u>When Heaven Invades Earth</u>

<u>If you enjoy this book go to ignitedhope.com</u>:

- ➢ For sermon downloads of messages by Steve & Wendy.
- ➢ To purchase books and resources.
- ➢ For information on the Backlund's speaking itinerary.
- ➢ To contact Steve or Wendy about speaking to your group.
- ➢ For many free helps to inspire your life.

Other Books by Steve Backlund

<u>Igniting Faith in 40 Days</u> – Written with Wendy, this book is ideal for a 40-day negativity fast and to pour "spiritual gasoline" on your faith and hope.

<u>Cracks in the Foundation</u> – This writing examines the negative effects of religious tradition that neutralizes the power of God's promises. Its teachings will repair cracks in your faith foundation so that God can build something great through you.

<u>Possessing Joy</u> – The joy of the Lord is our strength, and a merry heart is like good medicine. God has called us to serve Him with gladness. This book will give you incredible keys to do so.

<u>Victorious Mindsets</u> – Steve reveals 50 different mindsets that every world-changer needs for victorious living. Examples of these are: *I don't walk in regret; My gift will make room for me; I can adapt well to varied people and situations; If I perish, I perish; I work with God, not for God; I encounter God by faith, not feelings;* and *I do small things in a great way.*

INTRODUCTION

You're Crazy if You <u>Don't</u> Talk to Yourself **has a tongue in cheek title that plays on the word "crazy."** Definitions for crazy include: foolish, silly, senseless, outrageous, ridiculous, bizarre, weird and zany. These words would seem appropriate for those who ignore the overwhelming biblical admonition to "speak life" on a regular basis.

We are not only to talk to ourselves, but we are also to talk to the things in our lives. *You're Crazy If You Don't Talk to Yourself* will open you up to a deep understanding of the power of words. This is a truth that cannot be ignored by those who desire increased personal victory and who want to ignite spiritual revival wherever they go. Certainly, this book is not a formula to be used apart from a surrendered life to Jesus; but when its principles are combined with other biblical truths and intimacy with God, then it will help you dramatically increase your "talents" as the Lord commands (see Matthew 25).

You can use this book in the following ways:

➢ Read it straight through to get saturated with the truth that LIFE IS IN THE POWER OF THE TONGUE.

➢ Read it as a daily devotional alone or with family members.

➢ Read it in a group by studying one chapter per week and then coming together for discussion.

Chapter One

Words Are
Powerful

WORDS ARE POWERFUL
LIFE IS IN THE POWER OF THE TONGUE

"Death and life *are* in the power of the tongue, And those who love it will eat its fruit" (Proverbs 18:21). "I have set before you life and death, blessing and cursing; therefore choose life, that both you and your descendants may live" (Deuteronomy 30:19).

Proverbs 18:21 is an incredible verse for anyone who wants to bring positive change to themselves and to their environment. Unfortunately, the emphasis of this passage has usually been on the tongue's ability to produce death rather than on its potential to produce life (just as those who preach from James 3 mainly focus on the negative effects of the tongue). The power of Proverbs 18:21 is this: **Life is in the power of the tongue.** Meditate on these words. Say them out loud. Join this with Romans 4:17 ("God, who gives life to the dead and calls those things which do not exist as though they did") for a key to seeing "dry bones" situations live (Ezekiel 37).

We certainly do not discount the destructive and hurtful effects of negative speech. Who among us has not been wounded or cursed by words spoken to us, especially by important people in our lives? Even so, it is best that we understand that God's positive is always greater than Satan's negative (see Romans 5:20). Just as "curse words" spoken can lock an individual or environment into an experience of restriction, chronic problems and lack; "life words" can become the catalyst for breakthrough, health, protection, spiritual revival and blessing in every way.

It is interesting that many have a political pro-life philosophy, but these same people unwittingly leave a trail of death behind them because of a lack of revelation about the power of words (for themselves, for others, for their surroundings, for their future, etc.). James 3:9-10 speaks of this when it says of the tongue, "With it we bless our God and Father, and with it we curse men, who have been made in the similitude of God. Out of the same mouth proceed blessing and cursing. My brethren, these things ought not to be so." In this passage, James refers to a person who is careless and does not understand that his words powerfully affect (curse) the people and situations of life. Truly, "these things ought not to be so."

Say it again: **Life is in the power of the tongue**. This truth is the central theme of the book you are reading. The Bible reinforces this reality over and over. It is one of the most profound spiritual laws in existence. Everyone who discovers this law will be like an investor who has learned about a foolproof investment. They will become the "those" in Proverbs 18:21, "And those who love it will eat its fruit." "Those" are people who love speaking life everywhere they go. They understand that fruit will come for the glory of God. They know that they are positively affecting the atmosphere of the spirit; thus, bringing life for themselves and their descendents. Let's become one of those and choose life. Truly, LIFE IS IN THE POWER OF THE TONGUE.

WORDS ARE POWERFUL
EVERY IDLE WORD

"But I say to you that for every idle word men may speak, they will give account of it in the day of judgment" (Matthew 12:36).

This passage should put a healthy fear in us; however, my fright in the past was not a positive thing. It was negative because it was rooted in a punishment mentality rather than from a deep concern of missing God's highest purpose for my life. (Remember, any time an apparent scriptural truth creates a fear of punishment for a Christian instead of hope, then our interpretation is most likely based on religious tradition and not on God's heart.)

If it is not for punishment, then why are we going to have to give account for every idle (careless) word that we speak? I believe that this giving account will be the revelation of how all our words impacted the spirit realm and then ultimately the physical realm. We'll see images of how an off-handed comment of blessing sent angels scurrying to release that blessing, or how a self-debasing statement put boundaries on our lives and gave permission to the demonic realm to harass us. We will be amazed and perhaps say, "Was I that powerful? Did I actually have that much influence with what I said?" It will likely be a sobering time, and we will wish that we had another chance to speak life.

There is another way to look at this verse as well. It has to do with the time period we assume for the day of judgment. Traditional thinking concludes that it is after we die and go to heaven. I don't dispute the reality of that, but we also experience daily the judgment of whether we increase in the things of God or not. Our experience today is largely the result of choices we made yesterday, and our experience tomorrow will result from what we do today. Jesus taught this in Luke. "Judge not, and you shall not be judged. Condemn not, and you shall not be condemned. Forgive, and you will be forgiven. Give, and it will be given to you: good measure, pressed down, shaken together, and running over will be put into your bosom. For with the same measure that you use, it will be measured back to you" (Luke 6:36-38). We see here that in many ways what life gives us is proportional to what we have given in the past – whether good or bad. (It is the law of sowing and reaping as described in Galatians 6:7-9.) In this sense, we experience a judgment that brings freedom or restriction. It is the wise person who "gives an account" to himself by seeing past spoken words as a major contributing factor in his current situation. This will create a sense of dominion in his spirit and propel him to speak life instead of death in the future.

Right now, let's renounce the habit of speaking idle words that bring a negative judgment to our lives. We will be happy we did. Truly, LIFE IS IN THE POWER OF THE TONGUE.

WORDS ARE POWERFUL
JUSTIFIED BY OUR WORDS

"For by your words you will be justified, and by your words you will be condemned" (Matthew 12:37).

When Jesus said that words would be the deciding factor in whether we are justified or condemned, He certainly was not saying that our choice of words would decide whether we go to heaven or hell. We know from scripture that heaven was earned only by Jesus' sinless life, and it is faith in His finished work that grants us heaven. Nobody will gain entrance into heaven by being good enough in word or deed, so **we can conclude that Jesus is not talking about our eternal destiny when He says we will be justified or condemned by our words. So then, what is He referring to?**

Consider this: When a building is condemned, it is deemed unfit to be used. It is not safe. It needs repair before it can once again be used for its intended purpose. This is similar to our lives. Who among us has not "condemned" areas of our lives by a spoken word? Just as the children of Israel did in the Old Testament, we can doom ourselves to wilderness living because of words spoken (see Numbers 13 and 14).

The word justified sheds further light on this. It means to be right, vindicated, correct and within our rights. Faith in Jesus justifies us to receive and partake of all that He won on the cross (forgiveness, eternal life, righteousness, health, abundant provision, protection and blessing in every way). We are within our rights to claim all these things for ourselves. We are vindicated from every lawful reason that would say we are not entitled to them. That is something to shout "Glory" about! Some might say as they hear this, "This is all great, but what do our words have to do with being justified?"

Our tongue is the rudder for our lives (James 3:3-5). Also, the Bible says, "Confession is made unto salvation" (Romans 10:10). We could not get saved until we confessed Jesus as Lord. This declaration took what was available to us and made it legally ours. Our confession justified us to receive what was within our rights to receive. What was true for our salvation is also true for each area of life where Christ won the victory. Instead of being condemned to futility, we have the privilege of justifying our receiving each aspect of the abundant life that Jesus has provided for us. The wise Christian says, "I receive right now Jesus as my healer, as my deliverer, as my abundant provider" and so on. At the moment of proclamation, we receive that specific benefit into our life, and then we start contending for its full manifestation.

Wow, it is truly powerful when Jesus said, "For by your words you will be justified, and by your words you will be condemned." Let's not condemn our lives to being unfit to be used, but let's speak forth God's exceedingly great and precious promises to experience all that Jesus has justified for us, in us and through us. Truly, LIFE IS IN THE POWER OF THE TONGUE.

WORDS ARE POWERFUL
BRINGING ORDER TO DISORDER

"In the beginning God created the heavens and the earth. The earth was without form, and void; and darkness *was* on the face of the deep. And the Spirit of God was hovering over the face of the waters. **Then God said**, 'Let there be light'; and there was light. And God saw the light, that *it was* good" (Genesis 1:1-4).

How do we bring order to disorder? How do we bring life to dead places? How can we influence the future order in the lives of our children? What gives the Spirit of God something to work with so that God's purposes can be accomplished and His victory released into lives and circumstances? To answer these powerful questions, it is instructional to go back to the beginning and see how God created life in His world. In Genesis 1, the Spirit was hovering over substance that was useless and chaotic. The Spirit saw the potential that was there but was unable to bring change unless given something to work with. That "something" was God's words, "Let there be light." Once spoken, the Spirit was empowered to bring order and life to earth and the universe.

We receive further insight in Hebrews 11:3, "the worlds were framed by the word of God." "Framed" means "to mend what has been broken, to repair, to complete and to put in order." This verse ends with the phrase, "so that the things which are seen were not made of things which are visible." **The natural realm results from things that happen first in the spiritual realm.** Just as Jesus' cursing of the fig tree first affected the unseen roots in Mark 11, so our words affect the spirit realm and eventually impact life on earth. We give the Holy Spirit something to work with to bring order and to repair what's been broken.

Romans 4:17 says, "God, who gives life to the dead and calls those things which do not exist as though they did." This passage is referring to Abraham who had his name changed from Abram to Abraham (which means "father of a multitude"). He was to "call those things which did not exist (his uncountable descendents) as though they did." The Spirit was hovering over His promise for twenty-four years before He really had something to work with in Abraham's confession. One year after he started calling himself by God's promise, Isaac was born and Abraham's avalanche of offspring began.

So how about you? You are made in the image of God. Are you giving the Holy Spirit something to work with on a regular basis so that order and repair can come to your life, to your family, to your church, to your city and beyond? God framed His future by speaking, "Let there be light." That word is still working. (Scientists say the universe is still expanding.) Let's frame our future by doing what God does to bring life to dead places – "calling those things that do not exist as though they did." Truly, LIFE IS IN THE POWER OF THE TONGUE.

WORDS ARE POWERFUL
WORDS CAN "BRIDLE" OUR FUTURE

"My brethren, let not many of you become teachers, knowing that we shall receive a stricter judgment. For we all stumble in many things. If anyone does not stumble in word, he *is* a perfect man, able also to bridle the whole body" (James 3:1-2).

Like many passages in the Bible, these verses in James formerly made me fearful and hopeless. Now they fill me with eager anticipation because the positive message that is contained in them is much greater than the perceived negative.

My former punishment-mentality viewed these verses as follows: First, I thought that teachers/leaders better not do anything wrong or else punishment would await them in heaven. This "truth" did not free me, but bound me up. Certainly we cannot discount the awesome responsibility of leadership because it is foolish to lead with words only and not first with lifestyle. It is also unwise to not recognize that leaders are more responsible for their words because of the greater authority their words carry in the

13

spirit realm because of their position. Even so, I Timothy 3:1 says, "This *is* a faithful saying: If a man desires the position of a bishop, he desires a good work." It is God's heart for us to yearn to grow into a place of profoundly influencing others; and the bridling of the tongue is vital to doing so successfully. Secondly, I wrongly believed that James 3:2 was proclaiming, "We all sin in many ways, but we especially sin with our words and that is the way it will always be." This lie was seemingly reinforced by James 3:8, "No man can tame the tongue."

What then is in these verses that ignites such hope? Look again at this phrase, "If anyone does not stumble in word, he is a perfect man, able also to bridle (control) the whole body." Yes, James says, "No man can tame the tongue," but we are no longer "mere men" in Christ. We are a new creation able to do all things through Christ who strengthens us (2 Corinthians 5:17; Philippians 4:13). **James is saying that transforming our words will bring a corresponding transformation to the particular part of our life that we are speaking about.** Joel 3:10 says, "Let the weak say, 'I am strong.'" We don't deny weakness, but part of walking in strength is to say we are strong before we feel or seem strong. This spoken word about strength "bridles" the whole body toward power instead of weakness. This is a remarkable truth that applies to every area of life.

Let's look at one final thing about James 3:1-2. The teacher mentioned in verse one would do well to focus more on his words outside of the teaching setting than he does when he is teaching others. **If he regularly speaks life in daily circumstances, he will have no problem releasing life in his teaching.** He will develop into the perfect man of verse two by bridling his tongue on an increasing basis. (The word perfect here actually means "mature" and "whole.")

So what are we waiting for? Let's consistently declare truth about who God says we are, what He says we can do, and what He says we already have in Christ. It will bridle our lives into His great purposes. Yes, LIFE IS IN THE POWER OF THE TONGUE.

WORDS ARE POWERFUL
WORDS CAN SET OUR LIFE'S COURSE

James 3 is a gold mine of truth for those who want to understand that life is in the power of the tongue. James wrote that if we can bridle (control) our tongue, then we can "bridle the whole body" (verse 2). He goes on to compare the power of the tongue with the tremendous influencing capacity of a horse's bridle or a ship's rudder. He says, "Indeed, we put bits in horses' mouths that they may obey us, and we turn their whole body. Look also at ships: although they are so large and are driven by fierce winds, they are turned by a very small rudder wherever the pilot desires. Even so the tongue is a little member and boasts great things" (James 3:3-5).

The phrase "even so the tongue" should send positive shock waves through our souls. James is telling us that we can turn things in God's direction by walking in the revelation that life is in the power of the tongue. Unfortunately, James 3 has been mostly interpreted as a warning against the perils of negative speech. Yes, one ungodly word can spark a forest fire of problems, but there is something greater to see here. If we only focus on stopping wrong behavior, we will never really bring godly change. **Eliminating wrong words does not create life, but life is released by right words that are in agreement with God.** One spark of a spoken word can ignite a fire of revival.

Where do you want to be in one year, five years or in twenty years? What promises has God given you? What prophetic words have been repeatedly spoken over you? It is important that you start making declarations about these so that the ship of your life may move toward your prophetic destiny. **Our words are a rudder that takes us toward what we speak.** The ship of Abram's life dramatically changed course when his name was changed to Abraham (meaning "father of a multitude") at age 99. This provided booster power toward the fulfillment of the promise given twenty-four years earlier that said his descendents would be unimaginably numerous. He regularly declared the promise in his name, "I am father of a multitude" (Romans 4:17). This became the rudder to fulfill God's destiny for him.

15

I have tried to live in this principle for many years. I proclaimed, "I write books" long before I ever actually wrote one. There have been many other areas where my declaration took me to realities that I never before thought I could reach. Praise God!

Say these words, "Even so the tongue." Say it again. These are words that every world changer needs to have etched on the back of their eyelids. Where we go in life will depend on it.

If something significant is going to happen in the kingdom of God, a declaration must be made. Know this: If something happened, something was spoken. (And this speaking probably seemed insignificant at first.) "For who has despised the day of small things?" (Zechariah 4:10). Zechariah spoke this to those who were involved in the rebuilding of the temple. It was an exhortation to not minimize small beginnings. We, too, cannot underestimate the importance of the little things we do in obedience to God. (A walk of a thousand miles starts with a single step.)

Why do so many of us think that a negative word can do more damage than the benefits of a positive word? It is because we don't understand who God created us to be. We often don't comprehend that we have authority to start kingdom-advancing fires in the spirit realm through speaking life. We tend to think, "What possible change can I make to this huge forest that is spiritually dead?" God though asks us, "Can this dampened forest be ignited into spiritual fire?" He knows the answer, but like Ezekiel, He wants to see if we know who we are so that we can have the right answer (see Ezekiel 37). If we do, we will declare life (and change spiritual atmospheres) by speaking the promises of God. If we don't believe this, we will think that our little spark of a word cannot possibly even set a branch on fire, let alone a whole forest. This conclusion is a lie.

We are Holy Ghost arsonists. We can set fire to everything we speak life to. It may not seem much at first, but someone has to break out of the pack, go against the flow, speak hope where there seems to be no hope and "call those things that are not as though they are." Why not you? Truly, LIFE IS IN THE POWER OF THE TONGUE.

16

WORDS ARE POWERFUL
GRACE IS IMPARTED THROUGH SPEECH

"Let no corrupt word proceed out of your mouth, but what is good for necessary edification, that it may impart grace to the hearers" (Ephesians 4:29).

This is a great verse! We'll deal with "corrupt words" in our next section, but let's examine the subject of words that "impart grace to the hearers." Just as negative words can curse lives, godly words can bless the hearer (and empower the person to walk in grace and abundant provision). This imparted grace gives a supernatural ability to live in our divine nature (2 Peter 1:2-4). We truly bless people by saying words that give power to them to live as Christ lived.

This is why the gift of prophecy is to be desired above all gifts (see 1 Corinthians 12:7-11 and 1 Corinthians 14:1). New Testament prophecy is speaking life to people and situations (as illustrated in Ezekiel 37), and life must be spoken for it to manifest. Grace is not imparted through the ceasing of negative words; thus, the goal of our speech is more than just eliminating corrupt words that would proceed out of our mouths. Our aim is to embrace Hebrews 10:23-25, "**Let us hold fast the confession of our hope without wavering,** for He who promised *is* faithful. And let us consider one another in order to stir up love and good works, not forsaking the assembling of ourselves together, as *is* the manner of some, **but exhorting *one another*, and so much the more as you see the Day approaching**."

Let's look at each verse of this Hebrews passage for truth on the subject at hand. Verse 23 says, "Let us hold fast the confession of *our* hope without wavering, for He who promised *is* faithful." We are called to speak hope continually because hope is the soil that faith puts its roots in. Hope is the confident expectation that good is coming. We are to hold fast this confession. Note that it does not say to hold fast a thought or an idea, but a confession (something spoken).

Verse 24 – "And let us consider one another in order to stir up love and good works..." This consideration of others is needed

17

because what might impart grace to one won't necessarily do so for another. Athletic coaches understand this because they know that different players need different types of motivational words. We, too, must know this.

Verse 25 – "Not forsaking the assembling of ourselves together, as is the manner of some, but exhorting one another, and so much the more as you see the Day approaching." We are told to keep meeting with other believers so that we can consider what will encourage each one. This relational connection actually must increase as we see "the Day" approaching. It is because the last lap of our race here on earth must be fueled by an atmosphere of growing exhortation (encouragement). **We are to step up this verbal impartation of grace as we get closer to our finish line in life.** Human nature, though, would want to decrease positive words to others because of a tendency to grow weary of one another's faults. Because of this, many actually move into the deception of thinking they are successful in speech because they are not saying negative things. We cannot walk in this fraudulent thinking, but we are to move forward in imparting grace through various ways of encouragement to others. As we do, we will become like Barnabas (the "Son of Encouragement"), who was the catalyst in releasing the Apostle Paul into his ministry. To God be the glory! Truly, LIFE IS IN THE POWER OF THE TONGUE

Chapter Two

Overcoming

Word Curses

OVERCOMING WORD CURSES
WHY WAS ZACHARIAS MUTED?

"And the angel answered and said to him [Zacharias], 'I am Gabriel, who stands in the presence of God, and was sent to speak to you and bring you these glad tidings. <u>But behold, you will be mute and not able to speak until the day these things take place, because you did not believe my words which will be fulfilled in their own time</u>'" (Luke 1:19-20). "Now Joshua had commanded the people, saying, 'You shall not shout or make any noise with your voice, nor shall a word proceed out of your mouth, until the day I say to you, "Shout!" Then you shall shout'" (Joshua 6:10).

The silencing of Zacharias tells us much about the kingdom of God. What was his transgression that caused this consequence? Zacharias asked the angel about the feasibility of Elizabeth and him having a child at their age. The angel detected something in this questioning that threatened God's prophetic purposes. The solution to this was to hush Zacharias for the duration of the pregnancy.

Something similar happened in Joshua 6. The Children of Israel were about to conquer the first piece of their promised land (Jericho). To accomplish this, "General Joshua" gave a very unusual command. The people were to walk around the city <u>in silence</u>. No talking was allowed until the seventh day when they were to "shout the walls down." This unusual strategy was done because Joshua remembered that forty years earlier ten of the twelve spies spoke a contagiously bad report that led to forty years of wilderness living (see Numbers 13 and 14). As with the angel who was speaking to Zacharias, Joshua was not going to risk having <u>word curses</u> spoken that might hinder or stop the promises of God from being fulfilled.

James says this about the tongue, "With it we curse men" (James 3:9). A curse is a negative force that adversely affects individuals, families, groups of people and geographical locations. It is caused by a violation of a spiritual law or through words spoken. A simple biblical study reveals the power of curses (and, of course, blessings).

Jesus came to redeem us from the curse (Galatians 3:13-14), but we must receive this deliverance and blessing that He has provided. Many people (including Christians) unwittingly live under the shadow of word curses spoken by themselves or by others. Remember that James said, "With it [words] we curse men." One of these cursed men certainly can be our self.

We can hinder our lives through self-pronounced word curses when we make **concluding statements** like, "I am dumb"; "I cannot do that"; "I am accident prone"; "this will never change"; etc. These types of statements reflect that we don't understand how powerful we are. We carelessly speak and then find ourselves living in a prison of restriction and difficulty. "My brethren, these things ought not to be so" (James 3:10).

All overcoming Christians need to silence themselves from speaking word curses over their lives, others, their circumstances and their future. **This "negativity fast" does not mean we live in denial and never discuss difficulties, but it is a purposing to not speak out negative, unbelieving <u>conclusions</u> about these matters** (see below for insight on negativity fasts). Like Zacharias, let's ask God to give us a Holy Spirit zipper for our mouths so that we won't curse and abort the great things that have been conceived through prayer, faith, prophecy and obedience. Like Joshua, let's remind ourselves that if we cannot say anything good, then we need a new perspective before speaking anything at all. Remember, LIFE IS IN THE POWER OF THE TONGUE, so let's use our words to create blessings and not curses.

What is a Negativity Fast?

<u>What a Negativity Fast is Not:</u>
1. It is not denying that problems exist.
2. It is not "stuffing things" that are wrong.
3. It is not critical of others who may be struggling.
4. It is not irresponsible concerning things that need to be done.

<u>What a Negativity Fast Is</u>:
1. It is determining to focus more on God's promises than on problems.
2. It is learning to speak with hope about even the toughest of issues.
3. It is becoming solution focused rather than problem focused.
4. It is refraining from giving voice to pessimism, criticism of others, self-criticism and other forms of unbelief.
5. It is speaking about problems to the right people in the right way.
6. It is replacing negative words and thoughts with positive words and thoughts based on the promises of God.

Note: My book <u>Igniting Faith in 40 Days</u> is designed for a 40-day negativity fast.

OVERCOMING WORD CURSES
DEPOSITS INTO THE SPIRIT REALM

"Now there was a **famine** in the days of David for three years, year after year; and David inquired of the LORD. And the LORD answered, '*It is* **because of Saul** and *his* bloodthirsty house, because he killed the Gibeonites'" (2 Samuel 21:1).

We've talked about how certain words can create a curse either for ourselves or for others. Now we want to go deeper in understanding how deposits into the spirit realm eventually affect our life-experience in the physical realm.

A fascinating story is told in 2 Samuel 21. There was a three-year famine, and David was seeking to remedy it. We assume he did the normal things (prayer, repentance, etc.) to reverse this curse, but nothing worked. So he inquired further of the Lord, and he received this answer: "*It is* because of Saul and *his* bloodthirsty house, because he killed the Gibeonites." David's predecessor, Saul, made a bad decision concerning the Gibeonites. Saul's attitudes, words and actions cursed the spirit realm over Israel, and years later the people suffered the consequences. David had to renounce this sin and make restitution to the Gibeonites for blessing to come and the famine to end.

This is an astounding event that illustrates the reality of blessings and curses. Paul refers to this when he wrote, "<u>While we do not look at the things which are seen, but at the things which are not seen</u>. For the things which are seen *are* temporary, but the things which are not seen *are* eternal" (2 Corinthians 4:18). **If we want to make a lasting difference in life, we are to focus our prime attention on the unseen realm of the spirit.**

One of the ways we can heed Paul and look at things that are invisible is by stopping the flow of actions that produce curses. Like David, we need to ask God to reveal any spiritual root that is blocking blessing. For many, our Lord will reveal word curses as a cause of lack, chronic failure and "wilderness Christianity." (These words could have been spoken by ourselves or by a key person in our lives recently or long ago.)

As the Holy Spirit shows us curse-causing words, we renounce our agreement with these lies and come into harmony with who God says we are, with what God says we have and with what God says we can do. Then we can move forward in asking God for a greater revelation of the truth so we won't pollute our spiritual atmosphere with words that release a curse. When this happens, we can continue in the glorious journey of walking happily in knowing that LIFE IS IN THE POWER OF THE TONGUE.

OVERCOMING WORD CURSES
THE INFLUENCE OF WORDS SPOKEN TO US

"You are of *your* father the **devil**, and the desires of your father you want to do. He was a **murderer** from the beginning, and does not stand in the truth, because there is no truth in him. When he speaks a lie, he speaks from his own *resources,* for **he is a liar** and the father of it" (John 8:44).

"Then Jesus said to those Jews who believed Him, 'If you abide in My word, you are My disciples indeed. And you shall know the truth, and the truth shall make you free'" (John 8:31-32).

The truth will make us free. Conversely, the lie will enslave us. What we believe is the determining factor of whether our lives move forward or backward. We can have a "Super Christian" pray for us, but ultimately our own beliefs are the key to spiritual advancement. Yes, we need others to pray for us, but what we believe is ultimately more crucial to us and to our descendents.

Satan's lies can destroy ("murder") our potential. God's truth, however, causes us to soar spiritually. The voice we hear determines the direction of our lives and our progress in Christ.

Let's look at two verses about hearing that are vital to the formation of our beliefs. The first is Mark 4:24: "Take heed <u>what you hear</u>." The second is Luke 8:18: "Take heed <u>how you hear</u>." Mark's gospel reveals the importance of hearing godly, positive things rather than listening to sinful or unbelieving words (because our lives are largely shaped by the messages we allow ourselves to hear). This is so very true, but Jesus takes this to a higher level in Luke when He says, "Take heed how you hear."

There is a way to hear that will attract the supernatural, and there is a way to hear that limits God's flow of life and blessing to us. On many occasions Jesus spoke, "He who has ears to hear, let him hear." This command illustrates the need to become disciplined in our hearing so that we can discern the depth of potential in what is being said.

There are two simple phrases that will increase how we hear. The first is "I receive that." The second is "I don't receive that." We can use these phrases in our thoughts or speak them out in key situations. They help us to be careful "how we hear."

There are also two things that are necessary for words to have the optimum influence. The first is if the speaker has a high level of faith and authority in the words he speaks. The second is a strong belief concerning the speaker's authority by the one who hears. These ingredients create powerful hearing that can work in the negative or the positive. For instance, if an authority figure (parent, teacher, etc.) says, "You are stupid" or, conversely, "You have what it takes to be successful," then those words have the power to shape a life if they are received by the hearer.

There is a potent verse in Hebrews about mixing faith with something heard. "For indeed the gospel was preached to us as well as to them; but the word which they heard <u>did not profit them, not being mixed with faith in those who heard it</u>" (Hebrews 4:2). The Old Testament saints heard the gospel (good news), but they really did not "hear" it. It is the same for many today.

Every day there are powerful promises being spoken forth, but faith is often absent and there is no profit to what was declared. It is the wise Christian who enthusiastically proclaims when hearing a testimony or a promise, "I receive that for myself" or "That's true" or "God will do it again." It is also the prudent person who (when hearing words that could curse or lower our expectation concerning God) says, "I don't receive that" or ""I do not come into agreement with that."

We will speak later of the benefits of the hearing of faith; but as we conclude this teaching today, I urge you to renounce any agreement that you have with a lie that has been spoken to you or about you. **Pray this prayer with me**: "Father, in Jesus' name, I renounce every lie spoken over me (that I have "mixed my faith with") which has cursed my life in any way. I also thank you that you will show me any falsehoods that I need to specifically deal with through prayer and through abiding in Your truth."

In conclusion, there are words that we hear that must be resisted, and there are words that must be grabbed hold of with zealous hearing. Our future (and our descendants' futures) depends a lot on our level of hearing. We can break curses off of our lives by unmixing our faith (our agreement) with lies and then intentionally mixing our beliefs with the good news of God's truth. Let's do this so that we can move full steam ahead in believing that LIFE IS IN THE POWER OF THE TONGUE.

OVERCOMING WORD CURSES
CORRUPTING WORDS

"Let no corrupt word proceed out of your mouth, but what is good for necessary edification, that it may **impart grace to the hearers**" (Ephesians 4:29).

This passage implores us to be very careful in what we say because our words are powerful. *Corrupt* means "rotten or putrefied." Corruption creates death and not life. Have you ever seen how one rotten piece of fruit in a basket can cause decay in the whole basket? Words are the same way. They can cause decay and death to dreams and potential if the hearer does not "take captive" (remove) the lie that was spoken (2 Corinthians 10:5). Those who are on the journey of speaking life need to be fully convinced of this.

Our words have the ability to impart decay (death) or grace (life). This impartation is like an intravenous spiritual tube to lives. Words that we mix our faith with cause a deposit into either a "grace container" or into a "curse container." These then feed into our lives the substances of life or decomposition. It is glorious to know that one God-inspired word can create a tremendous flow of life, but it's sobering to also realize one corrupt word can create big problems for those who hear a lie and believe it is truth.

In this section of this book, I am seeking to eliminate the effect of past words on our current mindsets and situations. We also want to impart revelation knowledge so that we will drastically decrease or eradicate the deposits of corruption that influence our lives. Here are some steps that you can take to accomplish this:

1. Re-read this chapter's teachings.
2. Prayerfully consider every area in your life that seems hopeless. Ask the Holy Spirit to show you any "corrupt words" that have been spoken over you that may be contributing to this sense of hopelessness. (These words could have been spoken by others or by you.)
3. Write down what the Lord shows you.
4. Press into God for revelation of the "kingpin" lie that seems to be the main source of the hopelessness.
5. Renounce that lie in the name of Jesus and speak the truth over yourself in that area so that grace can begin to be imparted to your life. Find others who have overcome this lie and ask them to speak their testimony over you (and to pray over you). Mix your faith with what you hear.

6. Make a list of declarations that you can proclaim morning and night (truths from God's Word and personal promises you have been given) so that grace can be imparted to you on a regular basis.

OVERCOMING WORD CURSES
WHOSE REPORT WILL YOU BELIEVE?

"Then Caleb quieted the people before Moses, and said, 'Let us go up at once and take possession, for <u>we are well able to overcome</u> it.' But the men who had gone up with him said, '<u>We are not able to go up</u> against the people, for they *are* stronger than we.' And they gave the children of Israel a bad report of the land which they had spied out, saying, 'The land through which we have gone as spies *is* a land that devours its inhabitants'" (Numbers 13:30-32).

A truth of life is that **those who say they can, and those who say they can't, are both right**. In the story of the twelve spies in Numbers 13 & 14, we see this in action. Caleb said he could, and he eventually did (see the book of Joshua). The other ten spies said they couldn't, and they never did enter into the Promised Land (even though they were created to do so).

Like the spies, Christians are given glimpses into new dimensions of life that Jesus won on the cross for us (aspects of God's promises that seem too good to be true). When we see or hear of these possibilities, two voices start speaking inside of us. The first says, "You were created to experience that, and you will." The second says, "You are not able. It won't work for you. The obstacles are too big." There is a good report and a bad report that is available to put your faith in. Whichever voice we have been feeding the most will be the loudest and most believable (which will create our experience regarding that area of our spiritual life).

"And **they gave the children of Israel a bad report** of the land which they had spied out." This bad report was believed and spoken, and thus doomed them to what was not God's will for them. The unbelieving spies, instead of sharing just the <u>facts</u> about the giants in the land, spewed forth <u>conclusions</u> about their own abilities based on lies that elevated the problem above the

28

promises of God. (Among other things, they inaccurately said that they were only grasshoppers in stature against these giants.) This created a spirit of fear that brought forth multiple word curses that polluted the spiritual atmosphere and further compounded their situation. It was a <u>defining moment</u> for them that took their lives away from greatness, into mediocrity and into a spiritual wilderness.

All of us have **defining moments** like the twelve spies. Usually we don't know that we are in the middle of a defining moment when it appears before us. Our goal, therefore, is to become like the sons of Issachar "who had understanding of the times, to know what Israel ought to do" (1 Chronicles 12:32). As we increase our discernment, we will be much less likely to proclaim word curses over our lives and much more likely to speak forth God's highest will (just like Joshua and Caleb).

As we consider further the bad report that was believed, I wonder what would have happened if the children of Israel had truly repented (changed their beliefs) in the wilderness. Can we speculate that the 40 years would have been drastically reduced? Would the older generation have been allowed to go in with Caleb and Joshua? It is unclear because even Moses was not allowed in, but repenting for and renouncing past wrong beliefs and decisions will accelerate the advance of God's kingdom. It is the wise Christian who asks God to reveal crucial moments where he or she has believed a bad report and has then uttered <u>concluding words</u> that have held back God's best (words about our identity or God's ability). These can be spoken out of fear, bitterness or anger. It is good to cut off our agreement with these lies.

Finally, it is necessary to begin to ravenously feed our faith and starve our doubts so that we will be prepared for new opportunities that present themselves to us. Joshua and Caleb broke out of the pack by believing God for the miraculous and impossible. They thought differently than the rest. **They focused on and talked about God's promises, not about problems and limitations**. They were this way before they went to spy out the land, and therefore they were ready when their moment came. One of the main ways we can do this is by continually speaking life over our circumstances and ourselves. <u>It will prepare us for those incredible moments that are coming in the days ahead</u>. Truly, LIFE IS IN THE POWER OF THE TONGUE.

OVERCOMING WORD CURSES
SELF-IMPOSED WORD CURSES

"Pilate said to them, 'What then shall I do with Jesus who is called Christ?' *They* all said to him, 'Let Him be crucified!' Then the governor said, 'Why, what evil has He done?' But they cried out all the more, saying, 'Let Him be crucified!' When Pilate saw that he could not prevail at all, but rather *that* a tumult was rising, he took water and washed *his* hands before the multitude, saying, 'I am innocent of the blood of this just Person. You see *to it.*' <u>And all the people answered and said, 'His blood *be* on us and on our children</u>.' Then he released Barabbas to them; and when he had scourged Jesus, he delivered *Him* to be crucified" (Matthew 27:22-26).

The Jews foolishly placed a word curse on themselves at a crucial moment in their history. Not long after this, in 70 AD, Jerusalem was destroyed with many dying. Was there a connection between what the Jews told Pilate and what happened when Jerusalem was destroyed? It is hard not to think so.

It is wonderful that in Jesus we have been redeemed from the curse. Galatians 3:13-14 tells us that Jesus became a curse so that we would not have to experience cursed living. Even though this is so, we must at times renounce specific generational mindsets that attract the curse back to us. We have to renew our minds away from patterns of thinking that draw the enemy into our realms of living. We also need to not complicate the problem by pronouncing imprudent words over our lives (like the Jews did before Pilate and like we probably all have done).

We can move forward in this by becoming students of our words. We often say the strangest things. Have you ever asked yourself why we speak such things as:

➢   I am sick and tired of this
➢   This is killing me

30

- ➢ It drives me nuts
- ➢ I'm so stupid
- ➢ Shame on me
- ➢ Shame on you
- ➢ That scared me to death
- ➢ This is driving me crazy
- ➢ You make me sick
- ➢ I am ready for the funny farm
- ➢ I can't do anything right
- ➢ I just can't believe it
- ➢ Over my dead body

Are these sayings simply harmless expressions that only a legalistic wordmonger would even mention, or are they words that could actually impact us negatively in some way? It is an interesting question, isn't it?

Whatever your response is to that question, let me give you something to ponder: <u>Could it be that if we can freely say such things, then we must not believe we are as powerful as God says we are</u>? Could it reveal that our core beliefs cause us to think we are a pawn in God's big chess game and that we don't have the ability to alter what God has planned for us anyway?

Jesus said that we will give an account for every idle word that we speak (Matthew 12:36). This is not just a truth to evoke fear in us, but it is a truth to let us know that our words have tremendous influence. Again, only an individual who believes he is spiritually impotent would speak without careful reflection on the impact of the words spoken.

It is tough to speak on such matters because of the tendency to get all bound up concerning what we say. This propensity gets worse when we encounter self-appointed speech policemen in our midst who jump on every wrong thing said. Even though there are these risks, it would be wise to listen carefully to what we say and discontinue saying things that would indicate we don't believe we are powerful beings in Christ.

In closing, let me illustrate this further by addressing something that at first glance may not seem related to the topic at hand, but it really is. Have you ever considered the phrase "traveling mercies"? (This expression is often used as a form of blessing to those who are going on some sort of trip.) It certainly is not a word curse, but it does appear to reflect a wrong belief system. Do we need mercy when we travel? The definition of mercy is "to not get what we do deserve." Do we deserve accidents and problems when we journey to another place? No, in Jesus we have a covenant of blessing and protection, therefore proclaiming mercy would seem to indicate that we don't believe our covenant is as big as it is. The words we speak do reflect our core beliefs. "For out of the abundance of the heart the mouth speaks" (Matthew 12:34). So it is not just the negative influence of wrong words that we concern ourselves with, but, more importantly, we recognize that our words reflect our true beliefs. And it is our beliefs that will launch us or bind us.

Let's cut off the word curses, go on a negativity fast, and then speak life in everything we say. Truly, LIFE IS IN THE POWER OF THE TONGUE.

Chapter Three

Speaking to Your Soul

SPEAKING TO YOUR SOUL
GETTING ANGRY AT THE RIGHT THING

"And take the helmet of salvation, and the sword of the Spirit, which is the word of God" (Ephesians 6:17).

I remember playing football when I was a freshman in high school. I enjoyed football except for one thing – I didn't like physical contact. Also, "mean" and tough players intimidated me. During practice and games, I tried to avoid being hit as much as possible. This passive and defensive approach did not make me very successful as a football player, and it actually increased my likelihood of injury. It was not a pretty picture.

One day at practice everything changed. I cannot remember the specific details, but I do know that I came to a place where I had enough of being pushed around and living in fear. I got mad. It was an anger mainly directed at myself. **I made a decision on the inside of me that I was not going to take it anymore.** I started to be more aggressive and began bringing physical contact to the other players before they brought it to me. As I became more assertive, everything changed. I began to enjoy football very much and became a star defensive player. It was an important time in my life that helped me beyond athletics.

If you have not played football, you may not understand completely what I'm saying; but this is still a powerful truth for you in learning to overcome the lies and intimidation of the devil. <u>We must rise up and proclaim God's truth and tell Satan what we can do so that we are not continually pushed around by feelings and circumstances that seemingly confirm his lies.</u>

Ephesians 6:14-18 reveals the armor of God that is necessary for triumphant living. This armor includes one offensive weapon. It is "the sword of the Spirit which is the word of God." Isn't it interesting that it is called the word? It's not named "the thought," or "the writing," or something else; but it is the word (something that needs to be spoken).

A powerful thing happens when we are willing to speak out God's promises. As we do, we are taken to another level by declaring truth in opposition to negative feelings. To see the reality of this, try this: Ask a friend to count backward in their mind from ten to one. As they do, ask them to say their name out loud. What happened to the counting? If they are honest, they will tell you that they stopped counting when they spoke their name. What is the point to this? It is **this great reality:** Our thought patterns will change when we speak something different than that which we are thinking. And when we are speaking "the Word", it not only changes our thought patterns, but it activates our spiritual armor to become offensive and move us forward in the things of God.

Are you getting pushed around on the playing field of life? Are you trying to avoid getting "hit" by the devil? If so, the Bible says, "Be angry, and do not sin" (Ephesians 4:26). Rise up and let righteous anger work for you. Start proclaiming the promises of God. Make a list of faith declarations to say daily with boldness. As you do, you will find yourself speaking to your own soul and not so much to the devil – for **the devil is only empowered through our wrong beliefs.** So let's start "hitting" these lies and this hopelessness with God's Word. As we do, we will help ourselves and others win a great victory to the glory of God. LIFE IS IN THE POWER OF THE TONGUE!

SPEAKING TO YOUR SOUL
BLESS THE LORD, O MY SOUL

"Bless the LORD, **O my soul**; And all that is within me, *bless* His holy name! Bless the LORD, O my soul, And forget not all His benefits: Who forgives all your iniquities, Who heals all your diseases" (Psalm 103:1-3).

Psalm 103 is a magnificent portion of scripture. The psalmist is talking to his own soul and instructing it to "Bless the Lord" and to "forget not all His benefits." He calls himself to <u>a high priority</u> ("Bless the Lord"), to <u>an incredible passion</u> ("all that is within me") and to <u>a disciplined way of thinking</u> ("forget not all His benefits"). He understands the tendency to drift away in priority, passion and thoughts, so **he deals with this backsliding by talking to himself**. He may have appeared crazy to others in doing so, but certainly not to God.

Let's go deeper in this remarkable psalm. Again, he tells his soul to "Bless the Lord". We know that we can bless God through actions and attitudes, but **James 3:9 says we bless God through our words**. Our soul needs continual encouragement to vocally bless God. We can do this by focusing on Jesus and speaking to Him of His goodness and greatness. As we do, something wonderful happens. This is why worshipping in song is such an important part of our church meetings. (As we bless God in church, it will help us do so outside of the church walls as well.)

"And all that is within me, bless His holy name." **There must be a demand placed on us to have passion in our relationship with God**. It is necessary to overcome any tendency to be lukewarm in our blessing of God. Yes, there will be differences in our expressions of this, but "all that is within me" signifies that every part of our being will regularly glory in Jesus our Lord.

"Forget not all His benefits." **Can you imagine an employee being unaware of his benefit package at work**? What would you think if he paid thousands of dollars for doctor bills when he had insurance that would have paid for everything? You would think he was either foolish or ignorant. Just as this employee would need to learn about and remember his benefits, believers must pursue revelation of the payment that Christ has already made for us (especially in the two areas the psalmist lists: forgiveness for every sin and healing for every disease). Once we receive knowledge and understanding of these things, then we talk to our soul on a regular basis about them so we won't forget. This is why having declarations to speak daily is so important (see back of book for sample lists of faith declarations).

Psalm 103 is about a person speaking to himself. It is not about someone speaking to God or to people. It's a godly man speaking to himself. He's not crazy. It is okay to do so. As a matter of fact, it is necessary because if we don't, we would leave a major weapon against the enemy out of our arsenal.

Talk to yourself. It may take a while to get over your self-consciousness to do so, but the awkwardness will soon disappear. Develop your own way to do so. It may not sound just like the psalmist, but it will be good as long as it works for you. Remember, YOU'RE CRAZY IF YOU <u>DON'T</u> TALK TO YOURSELF!

SPEAKING TO YOUR SOUL
ATTACKING DOUBT

"If any of you lacks wisdom, let him ask of God, who gives to all liberally and without reproach, and it will be given to him. **But let him ask in faith, with no doubting**, for he who doubts is like a wave of the sea driven and tossed by the wind. For let not that man suppose that he will receive anything from the Lord; he is a double-minded man, unstable in all his ways" (James 1:5-8).

Have you ever doubted your salvation? I did often as a new believer. If I felt and acted saved, then I thought I was saved. If I didn't feel like a Christian or if my behavior was struggling, I thought I wasn't a Christian. I was double-minded, and it caused me much inner turmoil.

I remember hearing a story of a man who had a similar experience and how he overcame this doubt. He found a wooden stake and wrote the date that he received Christ on it. He then drove the stake into the ground in his back yard. Then every time Satan would attack him with doubt, he would say, "Devil, follow me. I want to show you something." He would then walk to the backyard and show the devil the stake with the specific date on it. After doing this for a while, the doubting left him.

Even though I did not drive a stake into my backyard, I followed this example and attacked my doubts with God's promises. I proclaimed that I had indeed become a Christian when I received Christ. I spoke out loud the Bible verses that stated this. I declared, "I'm saved not because I feel saved or act saved. I am saved because God says I am saved." It was a turning point process that has been duplicated in many other areas of my life.

All aspects of salvation are received by faith. Once we believe, we will experience Christ's salvation. **I had to believe I was saved to start acting saved. This is vital to understand.**

"Confession is made unto salvation" (Romans 10:10). I was not saved until I declared I was saved. And even though I was born again, I wasn't going to experience the power of my salvation unless I kept saying I was saved. **Removing this doubt about my salvation opened wide the flow of Christian grace into my life.** Again, how I dealt with this uncertainty and double-mindedness became a model for me concerning how to deal with doubt in multiple areas of my life.

Each new dimension of our Christian experience will open up to us when we release our faith through a confession that it is ours. For instance, when I received revelation that the Bible says we are anointed in Christ, I declared, "I am anointed." I am not anointed because I feel anointed or always manifest power, but I am because the Bible says I am. Negative feelings and circumstances will try to send me the message (with help from Satan) saying, "You are not anointed! There is no fruit of this in your life! You must wait for fruit before you can claim that!"

My response to that needs to be, "Ha, ha. That is a lie from the pit of hell. I do not receive that evil report." "Driving a stake" ultimately defeats this lie in my mind and heart by continually declaring that I became anointed when I confessed it. Even though it may take time to fully defeat this lie, <u>our experience will eventually catch up to our beliefs</u>. **God's pattern is this: believe and you will see, not see and then believe.**

Who do you think (and say) you are? You have two sources to draw your conclusion from – past experience or God's Word. Most people create their identity beliefs from their experience. They say they are who their experience (their past) says they are. If they have experienced weakness, they say they are weak. If they are walking in poverty, they say they are poor. The Bible though says, "Let the weak <u>say</u>, 'I am strong'" (Joel 3:10). We don't deny symptoms of weakness, but we must confess that we are strong because it is a means to experience regular strength in our lives. It is part of overcoming the tendency to doubt that we are strong or rich because of contrary experience or feelings. This overcoming will require us to talk at times sternly to our soul so that it will not forget the benefits of our salvation (Psalm 103:1-3).

We all need to defeat lies that fuel doubt and double-mindedness. One main way to do this is to talk to yourself regularly about truth. YOU'RE CRAZY IF YOU <u>DON'T</u> TALK TO YOURSELF! **Others may think you're nuts, but your soul will love you for it.**

SPEAKING TO YOUR SOUL
STRENGTHEN YOURSELF IN THE LORD

"Why are you cast down, O my soul? And *why* are you disquieted within me? Hope in God, for I shall yet praise Him *For* the help of His countenance" (Psalm 42:5).

David is our role model for speaking to self. He would have appeared crazy to many in today's society because of this. In Psalm 42, he asks his soul, "Why are you disquieted within me?" It is amazing that he carried on such a dialogue with himself. He not only asks the question, but he then tells his soul what to do, "Hope in God." Finally, he notifies his soul of what he will do, "I shall yet praise Him!" **Had David lost his marbles or had he found a major key for walking with God**? The answer now seems obvious to me. He illustrates a secret for successful living that we too need to implement. Let's learn how to do this in our own lives.

We start this journey of speaking to our soul by addressing small things first. Then when big challenges present themselves, we will have already established the habit of confronting discouragement through talking to ourselves. David certainly found this to be true in I Samuel 30 when his family and the families of his mighty men were kidnapped. His men were angry and wanted to stone him.

What did David do in the face of this negative circumstance? He "<u>strengthened himself</u> in the Lord" (I Samuel 30:6). Another translation says, "He encouraged himself in the Lord" (AKJV). Wow! What did he do? I believe he talked to his soul. I can see him declaring God's promises and revisiting past victories. "I have been delivered from the lion, the bear, Goliath, Saul and a host of other enemies. God will deliver me now. Soul, hope in God for I shall yet praise Him." Well, the story ends in victory. He wasn't stoned and the families were restored. Soon after this, David became king over all of Israel.

There are many times in life where we can't just think our way out of discouragement or mediocrity. Faith comes by hearing, not just thinking something (Romans 10:17). Jesus said that the "violent" are taking the kingdom by force (Matthew 11:12). Our most violent acts need to be directed at our soul's tendency to conclude truth and reality from feelings, experience and circumstances (instead of God's promises). Our prayer life needs to include times of "having it out" with ourselves. We need to rehearse past victories out loud, boldly proclaim the promises of God and remind ourselves verbally of previous things He has said. If we do so, we will be speaking life, and we will bring back that which appears to have been stolen from us.

David was alone when his men talked of stoning him. There was no worship music playing for him. There was no crowd saying how great he was. He had to face this crisis alone with God. Like David, each of us will have times when we feel very alone, when circumstances and feelings want to oppress us. In these times, our support system of people seems to have disappeared. We will be tempted to think that no one cares (not even God). These lonely times are most likely the "evil days" in which we are to stand with the full armor of God (Ephesians 6:13). Part of that armor is praying "always with all prayer and supplication in the Spirit" (verse 18). I believe this "all prayer" includes passionate, violent declarations and speaking truth that neutralizes our fear until that evil day passes. David had to do it and so will we.

When I say to speak violently to our souls, I am not talking about any kind of self-hatred. On the contrary, self-hatred is one of the first big giants to have it out with if we are going to be truly fruitful in Christ. It is surprising to some that our spiritual warfare (and our righteous anger) first must be waged against inner lies and the conclusions that we draw from them concerning ourselves, other people, our circumstances and our future. It is not "us" we are angry with, but it is our belief systems that bind us to futility and mediocrity.

Let's move beyond trying to simply think our way into victory. Let's strengthen ourselves in the Lord by talking strongly to our souls until we are once again "above and not beneath" the circumstance. You know what? YOU'RE CRAZY IF YOU <u>DON'T</u> TALK TO YOURSELF about matters like this.

SPEAKING TO YOUR SOUL
THE POWER OF VERBAL THANKSGIVING

"Be anxious for nothing, but in everything by prayer and supplication, **with thanksgiving**, let your requests be made known to God; and the peace of God, which surpasses all understanding, will guard your hearts and minds through Christ Jesus" (Philippians 4:6-7).

In this section of this book we are teaching on the topic of talking to our own souls. As we do, it is important for you to know that in my own experience I rarely, if ever, actually address my conversation to my soul. I have taken this principle and developed the habit of repeatedly speaking life to my soul in other ways. **Verbal thanksgiving** is an excellent way to do this.

In Philippians 4, we are commanded to not worry about anything. (Remember, God never commands something that He has not provided the grace for us to do.) We are told to release worry through a kind of prayer that has thanksgiving in it. The Apostle Paul goes on to say that the result of this will be that the worry is replaced by a supernatural peace that "will guard your hearts and minds through Christ Jesus." The key to this is these two words: <u>with thanksgiving</u>.

Many years ago, I heard the Spirit say to me about my prayer life, "Steve, you need to thank more in your prayer life. Your continual asking concerning certain matters reveals that you don't have any expectation that what you are praying about will happen. If you really believed, your emotional state would be different long after you pray, but it isn't." He went on to tell me that **what I believed <u>after</u> my petition of prayer was more important than what I believed during the prayer**. He said that the words "with thanksgiving" would allow me to walk this truth out in my life.

Here is a challenge for you that I believe will revolutionize your prayer life: Restructure the asking part of your prayer time by making it 90% thanking and declaring what God has already done. It is amazing how often we ask for things that we already have in Christ or that we have already asked for in the past and is in a "spiritual delivery truck" coming to us. **Can you imagine continually reordering items for which you have been given a tracking number** and that are on a delivery truck coming to you? That is what we often do in prayer. The discipline of thanksgiving regarding past prayers prayed (and concerning what we already have in Christ) will accelerate the delivery of God's promises into our lives and circumstances.

I spend time verbally thanking God as often as I can. I do so when I drive, when I am doing yard work and at other times. Yes, I participate in other types of prayer (soaking, listening, praise, intercession, adoration, laughter, prophetic acts, etc.), but I am particularly drawn to the prayer of thanksgiving. If you were with me, you would hear me regularly say things like:

➢ Thank you that my family is blessed & protected.

➢ Thank you that my relationship with _____ is being strengthened.

➢ Thank you that I walk in supernatural health and that _____ has been healed.

➢ Thank you that the church I attend is in revival and going to the next level in _____.

➢ Thank you that my city is strong in family life, schools, government, economy, businesses, public health, moral purity, safety and churches.

➢ Thank you for using me to consistently bring encounters with You to other people.

➢ Thank you that all my needs are being met according to your riches in glory.

> Thank you that my marriage is getting stronger and that my children are having regular encounters with you that cause them to succeed in every way in life.
> Thank you that I have wisdom concerning _____.
> Thank you for your hand being powerfully on the upcoming elections and that your purpose will be accomplished.
> Thank you that there is breakthrough in _____ that I prayed about yesterday.

As you pray in this manner regularly, you will increase your faith concerning each matter that you thank God for. Your soul will hear this thanksgiving and become more and more peaceful and victorious as a result. You will build up your faith muscle and be on top instead of underneath the circumstances of life. In doing so, you will be so convinced of this that you will tell others, "YOU'RE CRAZY IF YOU <u>DON'T</u> TALK TO YOURSELF."

SPEAKING TO YOUR SOUL
INNOVATIVE STRATEGIES

"Call to Me, and I will answer you, and show you great and mighty things, which you do not know" (Jeremiah 33:3).

The San Francisco 49ers have been my favorite pro football team for as long as I can remember. As with any sports franchise, there have been ups and downs in the team's success. There was, though, a lengthy time of high achievement that was ignited by Bill Walsh who coached the team from 1979 to 1988.

Walsh inherited a losing franchise that won only two games and lost fourteen in 1978. The 49ers repeated that record (2-14) in Walsh's first year in 1979. Things began to turn around when the team drafted a quarterback from Notre Dame named Joe Montana. He became the starting quarterback in the middle of the 1980 season. The 49ers went 6-6 that year and won the Super Bowl the next year. They went on to win two more Super Bowls under Walsh and were a powerhouse team into the mid 90's.

Bill Walsh was an innovative coach who changed the way the game was played. He introduced the "West Coast Offense" that featured short passes from the quarterback to his receivers.

He revolted against the traditional "run the ball first and pass if you need to" philosophy. He also was known for having a script of fifteen to twenty plays that he would use in the beginning part of the game. There were many other ways that he altered the way football was played and coached. He was a catalytic figure.

God has destined you and I to be innovative people and innovative leaders. He is inviting us to call on Him so that He can show us "great and mighty things, which [we] do not know." Each of us is to hear things from Him for us to know and do that which no one (as far as we understand) has ever done before. Just as Coach Walsh took an old game to a new level through novel ideas, we too must take normal living and ministry to higher altitudes through "scripting" the first part of our days with innovative steps. For me, God has shown me how speaking life to my soul in regular and creative ways is a key to revolutionizing my life and environments. **I am being shown to do things that I have not heard any person speak or write about.** I believe that you, too, can find new great and mighty ways to impart life to your soul for the days ahead. Ask God about it, and He will answer you.

As we conclude today's teaching, I want you to once again pray out loud "with thanksgiving" to our Lord in a way that will strengthen your soul. Declare out loud the following:

> ➤ Thank you for the great day I will have.
> ➤ Thank you for your anointing being strong in our church.
> ➤ Thank you for ministering to _____ that I prayed about yesterday.
> ➤ Thank you for the mountain of _____ that has been removed in the spirit realm, which I will see soon removed in the natural realm.
> ➤ Thank you that I consistently bring God encounters to other people.
> ➤ Thank you that this book is changing my life in positive ways. Thank you that I will never be the same again.

Chapter Four

Setting the Course Of Your Life

"For we all stumble in many things. If anyone does not stumble in word, he *is* a perfect man, able also to bridle the whole body. Indeed, we put bits in horses' mouths that they may obey us, and we turn their whole body. Look also at ships: although they are so large and are driven by fierce winds, they are turned by a very small rudder wherever the pilot desires. <u>Even so the tongue</u> is a little member and boasts great things. See how great a forest a little fire kindles!" (James 3:2-5).

Remember this powerful truth: <u>if something happened, then something was spoken</u>. God spoke the world into existence, and our present realities have been greatly influenced by words spoken in the past. Psalm 34:12-14 confirms this truth:

12 <u>"Who *is* the man *who* desires life,</u>

<u>And loves *many* days, that he may see good?</u>

13 Keep your tongue from evil,

And your lips from speaking deceit.

14 Depart from evil and do good;

Seek peace and pursue it."

David asks a question in verse twelve: "Who *is* the man *who* desires life, And loves *many* days, that he may see good?" He is basically asking, "Who wants a long, fulfilling and happy life?" The answer from most would be, "I do." What then does David first mention as apparently the most important factor in having this abundant life?

Before we answer that question, let's consider what he did not say. He did not mention different types of behaviors and attitudes. Nor did he promote the need for spiritual disciplines. What does he say then? <u>David tells us that we must first concentrate on the words we speak</u>. He basically says, "Don't speak evil and don't speak lies." One of the meanings for evil is "malignant." This compares to Ephesians 4:29, "Let no corrupt word proceed out of your mouth." (Remember, speaking corrupt or malignant words is not just cussing or gossiping. It is speaking death instead of life.)

We are also told to keep our lips from "speaking deceit."

This certainly would include refraining from dishonesty in the things we talk about, but there is a much deeper meaning. Do our words consistently line up with the lies of the devil or with the truths of God? If we see life through the "lens" of lies (the devil's perspective), we will "speak deceit" and curse our future. If we see life through God's perspective (truth), we will speak truth and bless our future.

We will talk more about setting the course of our lives through the words we speak; but as we close this devotional thought today, I want to give you some homework to help you apply the truths of today's lesson and the truths of this entire book so far.

1. Turn to the appendix and read out loud one or more of the **declarations lists**. Do this each day for the rest of the book.

2. **Start speaking life** over yourself and your circumstances like never before. Find the ideal times for you to do so (i.e. driving, cleaning house, in the bathroom, at the end of your prayer times, walking from room to room in your home, etc.). Point at things and declare the promises of God. It may take a while for you to get used to doing this, but it will soon become natural.

3. **Ask God for a heightened awareness of** when you speak deceit (when your words are in agreement with the **lies** of the devil and not God's truth). I remember when I first became aware of the lies I believed and spoke. It was at first depressing, but then it was empowering as I knew I could make the changes needed to reverse the curse.

Setting the Course of Our Life
CHANGING OUR LIFE'S DESTINATION

"Come, you children, listen to me; I will teach you the fear of the LORD. <u>Who *is* the man *who* desires life, And loves *many* days, that he may see good?</u> Keep your tongue from evil, And your lips from speaking deceit. Depart from evil and do good; Seek peace and pursue it" (Psalm 34:11-14).

"Therefore, my beloved, as you have always obeyed, not

as in my presence only, but now much more in my absence, **work out your own salvation with fear and trembling**" (Philippians 2:12).

David shows us an incredible way to think and live in Psalm 34. He invites us into an understanding of something very important. "Come, you children, listen to me; I will teach you the fear of the LORD." We know that the fear of the Lord is the beginning of wisdom and the beginning of knowledge (Proverbs 9:10 and Proverbs 1:7). This fear, though, is not a fear of punishment. (Jesus was punished for the believer.) Yes, we are to fear that we might drift away from God, but a greater dread for the Christian is to not reach our full potential or fruitfulness in Christ (and that we will stagnate into mediocrity, distraction and spiritual barrenness). I believe this fear is the same as the "fear and trembling" mentioned in Philippians 2:12, which will cause us to "work out" into our world the great salvation that is within us.

I propose that one of the first things we should fear is that we won't speak life and won't create an increasingly successful environment for our future and those connected to us. To avoid this mistake, we must realize the power of this statement: I set the course of my life through my words. Yes, there are many other factors in determining the course of our lives. But if we don't understand the power of our words, we will either be cursing the positive things we are doing, or we will miss creating opportunities because of our silence. This is unfortunate and too often true.

Our lives are like a huge ocean liner. If the course of a ship is changed by one degree when it is far from land, it will arrive in a much different spot than the original course would have taken it. Our declarations change the course of our lives now by small degrees, but what a difference it makes in our final destination (for us and our descendents).

I asked this question earlier, but where do you want to be in five years? Ten years? In 300 years (through your descendents)? Start declaring it now. Think long term. Proactively set the course of your life and family tree through calling those things that are not as though they are. It will be the rudder to your life. You won't be sorry.

YOU'RE CRAZY IF YOU <u>DON'T</u> TALK TO YOURSELF and to the things in your life.

Here are two things to do:

1. Read your declarations and continue speaking life throughout the day.

2. Start the habit today of proclaiming dreams you feel God has given you. Also, set the course of your life by declaring God's general promises and His specific ones that He has made real to you. Say things like, "I will . . . "; "I have . . . "; "My family is . . . "; "Thank you Jesus for . . . "; etc.

Setting the Course of Our Life
GOING AGAINST THE FLOW OF UNBELIEF

"Not that I have already attained, or am already perfected; but **I press on**, that I may lay hold of that for which Christ Jesus has also laid hold of me. Brethren, I do not count myself to have apprehended; but one thing *I do,* forgetting those things which are behind and **reaching forward** to those things which are ahead, I **press toward the goal** for the prize of the upward call of God in Christ Jesus" (Philippians 3:12-14).

Weight lifters understand that muscles are built by pressing against resistance. Overcoming Christians also understand that resistance is a friend in our journey to become fully convinced about God's goodness and His promises.

Salmon are a fascinating fish. They are birthed in fresh water, then live in the ocean for years, and finally come back to fresh water to spawn so that their species can increase in number. The remarkable thing about this process is that they spawn in the same location where they were born, and they often overcome great odds (waterfalls, etc.) to get there. God has put in them a homing device (direction) and an overcoming spirit to fulfill their calling. He has done the same for us.

"For this is the love of God, that we keep His commandments. And **His commandments are not burdensome**. For whatever is born of God <u>overcomes the world</u>. And this is the victory that has overcome the world—our faith" (I John 5:2-4). We also have what it takes to go upstream in life (against the resistance). Truly, the victorious Christian will embrace a life of swimming upstream against old "mind currents" that want to imprison them in valleys of unfruitfulness. One way to do this is by setting the course of our lives with words to go against the flow of unbelief.

Here are some common situations that often contain lies, which can be combated with a specific promise of God:

1. **When experiencing lack and uncertainty, say**, "My God will supply all my needs according to His riches in glory" (Philippians 1:9).

2. **When feeling hopeless, say**, "God has a way to get me from here to where I need to be. There is a direction for me to take that is powerful and good, and He will empower me to walk in it" (I Corinthians 10:13).

3. **When feeling weak, say**, "I can do all things through Him who strengthens me" (Philippians 4:13).

4. **When you think you are a failure, say**, "He who has begun a good work in [me] will complete it" (Philippians 1:6).

5. **When you don't know what else to do**, bottom line things and say, "I am going to be okay because my God will make things work out for me" (Romans 8:28).

These responses will help us set the course of our life toward God's Promised Land and away from mediocre or shipwrecked living. There have been seasons in my life where I have had to focus extra time in speaking and thinking God's promises. Remember, it is His promises that allow us to be "partakers of the divine nature" of supernatural living (2 Peter 1:4).

Spoken words have a powerful effect, but inner self talk is also important to our lives. We resist lies first in our thoughts. More on this ahead. In the meantime, remember, you might be crazy if you <u>don't</u> talk to yourself.

Setting the Course of Our Life
CHANGING OUR SELF-TALK

"Finally, brethren, whatever things are true, whatever

things *are* noble, whatever things *are* just, whatever things *are* pure, whatever things *are* lovely, whatever things *are* of good report, if *there is* any virtue and if *there is* anything praiseworthy—**meditate on these things**" (Philippians 4:8).

Spoken words have a powerful effect, but inner self-talk is also very important to our lives. We resist lies first in our thoughts. This inward conversation is what Paul refers to in Philippians 4:8. He urges us to intentionally direct our thoughts in specific directions ("meditate on <u>these</u> things"). It is a part of our spiritual warfare of "bringing every thought into captivity to the obedience of Christ" (2 Corinthians 10:5). **All believers must learn the habit of inwardly redirecting thoughts** toward faith, hope and love, and away from the lies that create hopelessness, fear, selfishness and ungodly priorities.

Self–talk refers to the dialogue that happens inside our head when we are faced with the challenges of life or even simple day-to-day matters. It is a running commentary in our thinking about everything we do. It never lets anything occur without meditation or reaching some sort of conclusion.

There are four main areas of life where this meditation (self-talk) takes place:

1. **<u>Conclusions About Our Self</u>** – Who do we think we are? We cannot use our experience or our feelings to conclude this. Joel says, "Let the weak say, 'I am strong'" (Joel 3:10). We are to create our identity beliefs from God's Word and not from our experience.

2. **<u>Conclusions About Others</u>** – The Bible says that love "believes all things, hopes all things" (I Corinthians 13:7). Our thoughts about others will either help release them into a higher place or become a hindrance in the spirit realm for them (especially if we are a person of influence in their lives). Even in times when we must confront difficult situations in relationships, we can still guard our hearts and seek to see the person as God sees them.

3. **<u>Conclusions About God</u>** – Just as we cannot create our identity beliefs from our experience, we cannot create our theology from it either. Our God-concept must be strongly

defended from demonic lies that raise doubts about God's will, His goodness, His power and the details of our salvation.

4. **Conclusions About Our Circumstances** – Hear this truth: **how we respond to what is happening is almost always more important than what is happening.** We must purpose to not place conclusions on circumstances without first meditating on the promises and goodness of God.

It is important to have special seasons in our lives where we declare war on our thoughts. It can indeed get pretty intense at times, but it will become easier as we develop new strongholds of faith, hope and love. So turn up the volume of your self-talk today by meditating (thinking) on God's promises, love and goodness like never before.

Setting the Course of Our Life
USING OUR SPIRITUAL RUDDER

"Look also at ships: although they are so large and are driven by fierce winds, they are turned by a very small rudder wherever the pilot desires. **Even so the tongue...**" (James 3:4-5).

A rudder gives direction to a ship. Even though it is small, it steers a large vessel whichever way it is turned. A powerful engine is of no value unless the rudder is working properly. Our tongue works like a rudder for us, taking us wherever our words are directed.

Let me ask again: What dreams do you have? What promises has God made real to you? What changes do you need to make to become the person you are destined to be? Where do you want to be in five years? How can you point the "ship" of your life in the direction of these goals? You do so by using your rudder (your words) to direct you toward God's highest purpose.

Words not only direct us, but unlike the rudder of a ship, they also create power to move us to our destination. Romans 10:10 says, "Confession is made unto salvation." Our verbal declaration takes us to salvation. Ephesians 4:29 reinforces this by saying good words impart grace to the hearers (and we are one of the hearers of our own words). Grace is the ability and power to do God's will.

The following declarations will <u>pull you toward</u> what is said:

1. I am debt free.
2. I lead someone to salvation every day.
3. My marriage is experiencing breakthrough.
4. I write books that are read around the world.
5. My church is strong and making a difference.
6. I consistently bring God encounters to other people.
7. I am free from addictions.
8. I love to exercise and eat right. I laugh 400 times a day.

We do set the course of our lives with our words. The moment we speak, we begin to be drawn toward it. Certainly there are other factors besides words that will influence our final destination, but we cannot minimize the importance of our proclamations. Remember, whatever we continuously talk about, we will begin seeing an increase of in our lives (whether it is revival, problems, God's promises, the untrustworthiness of people, etc.).

Each of us can consistently speak our own set of declarations that relate to our unique goals, dreams and promises; and we need some that seem ridiculous and laughable (Abraham sure did). **It is important to remember that we are not just pulling _ourselves_ toward these things, but we are pulling _our descendents_, too, into what is being declared.** Some of what we say will only be fulfilled through our lineage (both physical and spiritual).

So what are you waiting for? Start right now to point your life rudder toward what is good and what will make a difference for others. **Speak your future as if it is real now.** " . . . God, who gives life to the dead and calls those things which do not exist as though they did" (Romans 4:17).

COMMISSIONING ANGELS

There is a new breed of Christian who regularly talks to themselves and to the things in their lives. These have captured the heart of God's command to Joshua as he stood on the edge of his Promised Land, "**This Book of the Law shall not depart from your mouth**" (Joshua 1:8).

Joshua was not only building up his own faith through this constant speaking, but he was <u>commissioning</u> angelic beings to go before him on his behalf. "**Bless the LORD, you His angels, Who excel in strength, who do His word, Heeding the voice of His word**" (Psalm 103:20). Angels respond to the words of life spoken by us. When we speak God's promises and hope into situations, we give these angelic beings something to work with to accomplish God's will and promises.

Let me ask you a question: **Are angels primarily commissioned by our prayers or by our words**? It is a fascinating question that gets to the heart of what we really believe (and who we believe we are). Mark 11:22-24 helps us answer this. "**So Jesus answered and said to them, 'Have faith in God. For assuredly, I say to you, whoever <u>says</u> to this mountain, "Be removed and be cast into the sea," and does not doubt in his heart, but believes that those things he <u>says</u> will be done, he will have whatever he <u>says</u>. Therefore I say to you, whatever things you ask when you <u>pray</u>, believe that you receive *them,* and you will have *them.*'**" Note that the word "says" is mentioned three times and the word "pray" once in this passage. Prayer is important, but too often we cancel our prayer petition through <u>contrary spoken conclusions</u> after prayer. **Remember, what we say about a matter after we pray is just as important as what we say when we pray.**

I often wonder how many angels are commissioned by our words in prayer and then are stopped halfway to the answer by what we say later. (Is it possible that many angels live a herky jerky, unfulfilling existence?) Now I am not saying we can never discuss the negative facts of a situation after we pray, but I am saying that <u>spoken unbelieving conclusions</u> are a huge problem that can terminate the angel's assignment. That is an unfortunate reality of the spirit realm that would seem to happen far too often.

Our words set the course of our lives. It is the wise Christian who focuses on what they believe and say in times when God does not seem near. This is the time of real growth for us. It may be difficult to keep agreeing with our words for our past prayers and God's promises, but it will get easier through time. It will put us (and our descendents) on a course that will dramatically increase His kingdom coming and His will being done on earth as it is in heaven. Do you know what? YOU'RE CRAZY IF YOU <u>DON'T</u> TALK TO YOURSELF.

Chapter Five

The Hearing

Of Faith

THE HEARING OF FAITH
HEARING, NOT WORKS, IS THE KEY

"O foolish Galatians! . . . This only I want to learn from you: Did you receive the Spirit by the works of the law, or by the hearing of faith? Are you so foolish? Having begun in the Spirit, are you now being made perfect by the flesh? . . . Therefore He who **supplies the Spirit** to you and works **miracles** among you, *does He do it* by the works of the law, or by the hearing of faith?" (Galatians 3:1-5).

Paul presents two pathways for spiritual advancement and for the release of revival and the supernatural in our midst. The first option is "the works of the law." The second is "the hearing of faith." It is obvious from the message to the Galatians that the hearing of faith releases life while focusing on conduct (works) does not produce success, but actually curses us to be cut off from God's empowering grace (see Galatians 5:4-6).

It is interesting that Paul says the hearing of faith and not just faith. This is a confirmation of what is revealed in Romans 10:17. "So then faith *comes* by hearing, and hearing by the word of God." It is clear that there is a kind of hearing that accelerates kingdom life. Jesus said on many occasions, "He who has ears to hear, let him hear."

I want you to consider a question. What percentage of the normal Christian's effort to grow and change is focused upon altering conduct (works) and what percentage is placed on changing thoughts and beliefs (faith)? I have asked this question in various places, and I consistently hear that **the average Christian puts 70% to 90% of their emphasis on changing behavior and 10% to 30% on changing beliefs**. This is a disturbing reality that would elicit this statement from Paul, "Oh foolish Christians!"

Yes, we understand that every person has to address behavioral issues through wisdom, accountability and humility; but **the greatest way to change behaviors is by "the hearing of faith."** Our plan for Christian maturity must primarily include hearing testimonies, hearing truth, hearing God's love for us and hearing promises that will create a new wine skin of beliefs that will be able to contain the new wine of greater power, favor and abundance. This hearing can start by regularly speaking God's Word and promises. It is accelerated by repeatedly putting ourselves in environments that preach and teach faith, have frequent testimonies and encourage life-speaking declarations.

The hearing of faith is key for you today. Speak God's words so you can hear them. Imagine yourself being and doing what you say. See circumstances lining up with your words. Add a healthy dose of thanksgiving to your proclamations. Know that there will be a day soon when your heart's beliefs become fully convinced of what you are saying; and **then life won't just happen to you, but you will happen to life**.

THE HEARING OF FAITH
IT SHALL NOT DEPART FROM MY MOUTH

"This Book of the Law shall not depart from your mouth, but you shall meditate in it day and night, that you may observe to do according to all that is written in it. For then you will make your way prosperous, and then you will have good success" (Joshua 1:8).

The book of Joshua reveals the principles for victory and possessing God's promises. "After the death of Moses the servant of the LORD, it came to pass that the LORD spoke to Joshua the son of Nun, Moses' assistant, saying: 'Moses My servant is dead. Now therefore, arise, go over this Jordan, you and all this people, to the land which I am giving to them—the children of Israel. Every place that the sole of your foot will tread upon I have given you, as I said to Moses'" (Joshua 1:1-3). God said that He had both given and was giving them the land. (They had the land "legally," but they still had to move forward to occupy it.) It is the same for us today concerning such promises as walking in power, soundness of mind, health, abundance, evangelism and other areas. **Indeed, they are our possessions in Christ, but we need to contend for them to possess them in our experience.**

Understanding both the legal and experiential possession of God's promises is important as we consider the full implications of Joshua 1:8. Joshua, who was Moses' assistant, already had experienced deep intimacy and multiple encounters with God. He was now ready for the final preparation to lead God's people into their prophetic calling. He was repeatedly told, "Be strong and courageous," but God also said, "This book of the law shall not depart from your mouth." Notice that He said mouth, not heart or mind.

It is important to realize that the law is much more than commands; it is principles that govern life. These spiritual laws (like the law of gravity) can work for us or against us. Joshua was to talk to himself continually about the depth of God's commands. It is likely that this self-talk produced in Joshua the revelation that the people should not speak as they took steps to possess Jericho (Joshua 6). He realized that the law of words had been a significant factor in confining the previous generation to forty years in the wilderness. He was not going to have that happen again. (See also 2 Kings 18:36.)

Joshua 1:8 goes on to say, "But you shall meditate in it (the law) day and night." **One definition of meditate is to mutter**. Joshua was to speak under his breath of God's goodness, power, faithfulness and more. So are we.

The big question about all this talking to himself is "Why?" I believe the answer is wrapped up in the phrase, "the hearing of faith." He had to have a strategy to build strength and courage, and that strategy was to **speak words that would create a victorious belief system** that would cause him to succeed and be prosperous as an individual and leader.

If Joshua needed to do this before entering his Promised Land, we too will need to follow his example as we prepare for the next stage of our lives. Why not start right now to speak the amazing wonders of God's laws? Declare what you know to be true from God's Word. It is a big part of the hearing of faith. Let me tell you; YOU'RE CRAZY IF YOU DON'T TALK TO YOURSELF like Joshua did.

THE HEARING OF FAITH
INCREDIBLE, HIGH LEVEL HEARING

"Then He said to them, 'Take heed **what you hear**. With the same measure you use, it will be measured to you; and **to you who hear, more will be given**. For whoever has, to him more will be given; but whoever does not have, even what he has will be taken away from him'" (Mark 4:24-25).

Jesus calls us to carefully monitor what we **really hear**. This obviously includes gossip, profanity, slander and negativity; but this command is more about hearing the positive than it is about abstaining from the negative. **We are given an invitation here into a type of hearing that causes radical increase into our lives**. We are told that if we hear the right things, more will be given to us; however, if we fail to hear, then we will suffer loss of that which we already have. This is powerful and sobering to consider indeed.

Let's look at another verse about the kind of hearing that is catalytic to our future and to the furtherance of God's kingdom. "Therefore take heed **how you hear**. For whoever has, to him *more* will be given; and whoever does not have, even what he seems to have will be taken from him" (Luke 8:18). Jesus moves beyond discussing the contents of what we hear. He now tells us to **develop a method to carefully hear**. He says that it is not enough to simply hear something, but we must **really hear** it.

There are three things to conclude from the passages we are considering. First, we need to develop the habit of hearing the right things. Second, we must find a way to have an abundance of these words coming into our ears. Third, we need to develop the custom of hearing these words in an extraordinary manner – which is what would be termed as the hearing of faith.

The amount of our future resources is tied to our hearing. "With the same measure you use, it will be measured to you; and to you who hear, more will be given" (Mark 4:24). Here are some suggestions for increasing remarkable hearing (the hearing of faith):

1. Speak out loud God's promises and make declarations of

truth morning and evening (and throughout the day).

2. Take time to imagine these promises and declarations as true. "See" victory before it happens. This is one aspect of this higher level of hearing.

3. Remember recent prayers prayed (and declarations made). Verbally and specifically thank God for what He is doing in each thing prayed about or declared.

4. Know that every positive word heard is a seed of unlimited potential. **Determine to be good soil for these seeds through enthusiasm, agreement, personally receiving the word and by proclaiming later the key words heard and received.**

5. Ask God for revelation on what the hearing of faith is.

I urge you to reread and meditate on suggestion number four above. There is a gold mine in it if you can see it. Indeed, there are things being spoken around you right now that must be grabbed hold of. They might be nuggets spoken by a child or non-Christian. Or they could be new thoughts or dreams that you are muttering over yourself.

Start right now to allow the Holy Spirit to develop a high level of hearing in you. It is a key to where you are going. Oh, by the way, YOU'RE CRAZY IF YOU <u>DON'T</u> TALK TO YOURSELF.

THE HEARING OF FAITH
THE POWER OF SPEAKING SCRIPTURE

"For as the rain comes down, and the snow from heaven, And do not return there, But water the earth, And make it bring forth and bud, That it may give seed to the sower, And bread to the eater, So shall My word be that goes forth from My mouth. **It shall not return to Me void**, But it shall **accomplish** what I please, And it shall **prosper** *in the thing* for which I sent it" (Isaiah 55:10-11).

Scripture is a powerful force. "For the word of God *is* living and powerful, and sharper than any two-edged sword..." (Hebrews 4:12). There is no substitute for the words of the Bible in our lives. It does not matter how many great prophecies we get or how many fantastic Christian books we read; we must be people who are convinced that speaking Bible verses has a power far above other utterances.

Jesus spoke the Word in the wilderness when combating Satan's temptations. He did not just think it but spoke those passages that had been made real to Him. He said, "It is written" and then quoted Old Testament passages to disarm the devil (see Matthew 4). We too must get the Word in our mouth and declare it regularly. There is something that happens when we speak or verbally pray the scriptures. <u>You can't just think your way out of the wilderness, but the Word needs to be spoken</u>.

Here are some scriptural promises to speak. Read these out loud and memorize them. They are life changing.

➢ **I Have Supernatural Ability & Strength** – "I can do all things through Christ who strengthens me" (Philippians 4:13).

➢ **I Have Supernatural Hope and Open Doors** – "No temptation [trial] has overtaken [me] except such as is common to man; but God is faithful, who will not allow [me] to be tempted beyond what [I am] able, but with the temptation will also make the way of escape, that [I] may be able to bear it" (I Corinthians 10:13).

➢ **I Have a Supernatural Completion** – I am "confident of this very thing, that He who has begun a good work in [me] will complete it until the day of Jesus Christ" (Philippians 1:6).

➢ **I Have Supernatural Answered Prayer** – "Now this is the confidence that we have in Him, that if we ask anything according to His will, He hears us. And if we know that He hears us, whatever we ask, we know that we have the petitions that we have asked of Him" (I John 5:14,15).

➢ **I Have Supernatural Wisdom** – "If any of you lacks wisdom, let him ask of God, who gives to all liberally and without reproach, and it will be given to him" (James 1:5).

➢ **I Have Supernatural Provision** – "And my God shall supply all [my] need according to His riches in glory by Christ Jesus" (Philippians 4:19).

➢ **I Have a Supernatural Harvest Coming** – "He who sows bountifully will also reap bountifully" (2 Corinthians 9:6). "And let us not grow weary while doing good, for in due season we shall reap if we do not lose heart" (Galatians 6:9).

➤ **I Have Supernatural Assurance** – "And we know that all things work together for good to those who love God, to those who are the called according to His purpose" (Romans 8:28).

THE HEARING OF FAITH
SPEAKING RHEMA WORDS

"In the beginning was the Word, and the Word was with God, and the Word was God" (John 1:1).

"But He answered and said, 'It is written, "Man shall not live by bread alone, but by every word that proceeds from the mouth of God"'" (Matthew 4:4).

Let me give you an overly simplistic Greek lesson (yet it will help in getting an important point across). **The two main Greek words for "word" are *logos* and *rhema*.** Logos (which is used in John 1:1-3) refers to the entire Bible, while rhema is one verse from the Bible that God makes real to us as a personal promise or direction to take (Matthew 4:4).

We read the Word (logos) and receive illumination (rhema truths) that is to be used to resist the devil and to cause kingdom advancement. **The highest level of Bible reading causes us to know truth that will lead to increasing freedom.** "Then Jesus said to those Jews who believed Him, 'If you abide in My word, you are My disciples indeed. And you shall know the truth, and the truth shall make you free'" (John 8:31-32).

Jesus spoke rhema words in defeating the devil's lies in the wilderness (Matthew 4). He repeatedly said, "It is written" and then quoted the Old Testament. He had turned the logos into His personal rhema, and He used it at this crucial moment of His life.

I don't know what your concept is of how it looked when Jesus was talking to the devil in the wilderness. What do you think we would have seen if we were there? Would we have observed the devil in physical form? I doubt that because Jesus was tempted in the same manner we are tempted now. "For we do not have a High Priest who cannot sympathize with our weaknesses, but was in all *points* tempted as *we are*, *yet* without sin" (Hebrews 4:15). I believe Jesus appeared to be talking to Himself. We would have heard Him "speaking the Word." To the unenlightened, He might have appeared somewhat crazy.

Rhemas can come in a variety of ways. I remember a time of discouragement in ministry many years ago. As I was praying, I heard these words, "Steve, I have not called you to fail, but to succeed." This word was certainly supported by many biblical promises, and I was encouraged. It was, though, mainly a logos truth to my life. Soon after hearing this, I went to a ministers' prayer meeting where I shared my need for prayer concerning being discouraged. Hands were laid on me in prayer. The first person who prayed out loud said, "Father, I thank you that you have not called Steve to fail but to succeed." Bingo! **My logos was instantly turned into a rhema. It was one of the most important moments of my life.**

I began to use this phrase repeatedly against the lies of the enemy. I battled and overcame much of the temptation to doubt who God said I was and what He said I could do. **Like Jesus, I spoke out loud to an invisible force that was trying to steal my life.** I have spoken this rhema probably thousands of times. It has not only protected me but, more importantly, has launched me into really believing that I can succeed in all that is before me.

How do we get "rhemas"? Here are some suggestions:

1. **Read regularly the logos** of God's Word. Read the Bible (especially the New Testament).
2. **Note what stands out to you** – particularly truths and directions that are repeated.
3. **Meditate on and speak forth promises** you have been given (Bible verses and prophetic words about your life). Know that faith comes by hearing (Romans 10:17), so repeatedly speak and hear these.
4. **Write down** that which is most real to you and start resisting lies by speaking forth these truths as often as possible.

THE HEARING OF FAITH
TONGUES – "MORE THAN YOU ALL"

"**I thank my God I speak with tongues more than you all**" (I Corinthians 14:18). "He who speaks in a tongue edifies himself" (I Corinthians 14:4). "But you, beloved, building yourselves up on your most holy faith, praying in the Holy Spirit" (Jude 20).

The Apostle Paul makes a mind-blowing statement in I Corinthians 14:18. He says, "I speak with tongues more than you all." He was writing to the Corinthians, who were obviously no light weights in tongue speaking, but Paul said he did more. We realize that in I Corinthians he is primarily making the point that in church meetings it is better to "speak five words in the understanding than ten thousand in tongues," but in this discussion he also reveals a secret for strength as a Christian.

So here's a question: **When did Paul speak in tongues in such quantity?** Obviously, it was not when he was in public meetings, so he must have prayed "in the spirit" (tongues) frequently alone (in personal prayer, while he walked from place to place, while he worked on tents, etc.). He apparently was a constant tongue speaker. Could it be that people thought he was CRAZY because he was talking to himself so much in tongues?

It is important to know that there are two main purposes for the gift of tongues. The first is for the edification of the church meeting and its attendees. This occurs when an individual speaks a message in tongues, and then it is "interpreted" so that it can be understood by those present. The second purpose is for personal edification. Paul speaks of this in I Corinthians 14:4 ("He who speaks in a tongue edifies himself"), and it is confirmed in Jude 20 where we are told that our faith is built up by "praying in the Holy Spirit" (which is speaking in tongues – see I Corinthians 14:14-15). **This second reason of strengthening self is at the heart of Paul's frequent "tongue-fests."**

Paul spoke in tongues intentionally and with purpose. It was a key component of his growth plan for life and ministry. He knew that tongues edified him and built him up in his faith. He recognized that "faith comes by hearing," and a big part of this hearing was speaking in tongues. It is the same for us today.

We don't completely understand it, but something powerful happens to us when our soul hears us praying in the spirit. I believe there is a unique aspect to the hearing of faith for those who speak in tongues by faith.

The gift of tongues is for everyone and not just for a select few. Time does not allow for a detailed doctrinal teaching on why this is so, but one thing noteworthy is Paul's words, "I wish you all spoke with tongues" (I Corinthians 14:5). Also, even though we may not all operate in the public gift of tongues (I Corinthians 12:30), we all can (and I believe need) to pray in the spirit as much as we can.

If you don't currently speak in tongues, I urge you to pursue those who can help you in launching this experience. It is vital to the hearing of faith. If you do speak in tongues, then "turn it up" to the next level. Experiment with new dimensions in your prayer language. Find others who delight in speaking in tongues and encourage each other to be faithful.

Let's make it our goal to be like Paul and be able to say, "I thank my God I speak with tongues more than you all." We may seem somewhat CRAZY to others, but we won't be crazy to God.

Chapter Six

Speaking

To Things

Speaking to Things
Praying or Declaring

"Then He arose and rebuked the wind, and said to the sea, 'Peace, be still!' And the wind ceased and there was a great calm. But He said to them, 'Why are you so fearful? How *is it* that you have no faith?'" (Mark 4:39-40).

Jesus regularly spoke to things and, as we shall see, He tells us to do the same. **We know we have turned a major corner in our lives when we increasingly speak to things and decreasingly ask God to do those things**. This transition in our prayer life is not about ordering God to do things, but it is about our understanding the authority that has been delegated to us.

The story of Jesus calming the storm in Mark 4 is fascinating. If you read the entire account, you will find that **the disciples blamed a sleeping Jesus for their problems**. After they woke Jesus, they "prayed" to Him to help them. The Master spoke to the storm, and it ceased. This would seem to be a wonderful example of answered prayer, but Jesus ruins the celebration by implying that they should not have needed to get Him involved. He asked, "How is it that you have no faith?"

Say what? "Uh, Jesus, let me help You understand something. We did have faith – faith that You would take care of things. Our faith is what caused us to cry out to You to help us! What do You mean we have no faith?"

When Jesus asked, "How is it that you have no faith," He was implying that the disciples weren't getting what He had been saying to them in the past. It is one thing to have faith that God can do something, it is quite another to believe that we can do the same thing in His name. **It is not so much faith in God's ability, but in our ability in Christ.**

There is another story in Mark 11 that will help us in this discussion. "In response Jesus said to it (the fig tree), 'let no one eat fruit from you ever again.' And His disciples heard *it*... Now in the morning, as they passed by, they saw the fig tree dried up from the roots. And Peter, remembering, said to Him, 'Rabbi, look! The fig tree which You cursed has withered away.' So Jesus answered and said to them, 'Have faith in God. For assuredly, I say to you, whoever says to this mountain, "Be removed and be cast into the sea," and does not doubt in his heart, but believes that those things he says will be done, he will have whatever he says'" (Mark 11:14-23).

In this situation, Jesus spoke to a fig tree with a powerful result. (We'll discuss this more later.) When He was questioned about it, He started His answer by saying, "Have faith in God," and then made it clear that we should also be speaking to things ("mountains"). The phrase "Have faith in God" could just as easily have been translated "Have God's faith" (and actually is in certain translations). This rendition would seem to more clearly tie His cursing of the tree to His words concerning what we can do if we speak to objects in faith ("<u>whoever</u> says to this mountain . . .").

Can you imagine a police officer constantly asking his sergeant to do what the officer was commissioned to do? "Hi Sarge, this is Steve again. I have a person down here on 5th and Main that needs to be arrested. Could you come and arrest him?" The sergeant would say something like, "Oh you of little faith. Don't you know who you are? You have a badge and you have been commissioned to do this yourself. You don't need me to come down there. Please believe in who you are!"

Many of us are like that police officer, but we can break out of this wrong thinking by learning to speak to that which is around us. Doing so is a wonderful key to a higher level of living. YOU'RE CRAZY IF YOU <u>DON'T</u> TALK TO YOURSELF and to the things in your life.

Speaking to Things
Talking to Things – The Bible Way

Let's look at biblical examples of people talking to things:

1. <u>Jesus said (to the leper), "Be cleansed"</u> (Matthew 8:3).
2. The Centurion said, "But <u>only speak a word</u>, and my servant will be healed" (Matthew 8:8).
3. "And He cast out the spirits <u>with a word</u>, and healed all who were sick" (Matthew 8:16).

4. "He said to the paralytic, 'Arise, take up your bed, and go to your house.' And he arose and departed to his house" (Matthew 9:6-7).

5. "Then He said to the man, 'Stretch out your hand.' And he stretched it out, and it was restored as whole as the other" (Matthew 12:13).

6. "And Jesus rebuked the demon, and it came out of him; and the child was cured from that very hour" (Matthew 17:18).

7. "I am willing; be cleansed.' As soon as He had spoken, immediately the leprosy left him, and he was cleansed" (Mark 1:41-42).

8. "Then He arose and rebuked the wind, and said to the sea, 'Peace, be still!'" (Mark 4:39).

9. "Then He took the child by the hand, and said to her, 'Talitha, cumi,' which is translated, 'Little girl, I say to you, arise.' Immediately the girl arose and walked" (Mark 5:41-42).

10. "Then, looking up to heaven, He sighed, and said to him, 'Ephphatha,' that is, 'Be opened.' Immediately his ears were opened, and the impediment of his tongue was loosed, and he spoke plainly" (Mark 7:34-35).

11. "He rebuked the unclean spirit, saying to it, 'Deaf and dumb spirit, I command you, come out of him and enter him no more!'" (Mark 9:25).

12. "In response Jesus said to [the fig tree], 'Let no one eat fruit from you ever again'" (Mark 11:14).

13. "I say to you, whoever says to this mountain, 'Be removed and be cast into the sea,' and does not doubt in his heart, but believes that those things he says will be done, he will have whatever he says" (Mark 11:23).

14. "So He stood over her and rebuked the fever, and it left her. And immediately she arose and served them" (Luke 4:39).

15. "Then He came and touched the open coffin, and those who carried him stood still. And He said, 'Young man, I say to you, arise'" (Luke 7:14).

16. "Then He arose and rebuked the wind and the raging of the water. And they ceased, and there was a calm" (Luke 8:24).

17. "But He put them all outside, took her by the hand and called, <u>saying</u>, 'Little girl, arise'" (Luke 8:54).

18. "And the apostles said to the Lord, 'Increase our faith.' So the Lord said, 'If you have faith as a mustard seed, you can <u>say</u> to this mulberry tree, "Be pulled up by the roots and be planted in the sea," and it would obey you'" (Luke 17:5-6).

19. "And fixing his eyes on him, with John, Peter said, 'Look at us.' So he gave them his attention, expecting to receive something from them. Then <u>Peter said</u>, 'Silver and gold I do not have, but what I do have I give you: In the name of Jesus Christ of Nazareth, rise up and walk'" (Acts 3:4-6).

20. "<u>And Ananias... said</u>, 'Brother Saul, the Lord Jesus, who appeared to you on the road as you came, has sent me that you may receive your sight and be filled with the Holy Spirit.' Immediately there fell from his eyes *something* like scales, and he received his sight at once; and he arose and was baptized" (Acts 9:17-18).

21. "And <u>Peter said</u> to him, 'Aeneas, Jesus the Christ heals you. Arise and make your bed.' Then he arose immediately. So all who dwelt at Lydda and Sharon saw him and turned to the Lord" (Acts 9:34-35).

22. "But Peter put them all out, and knelt down and prayed. And turning to the body <u>he said</u>, 'Tabitha, arise.' And she opened her eyes, and when she saw Peter she sat up" (Acts 9:40).

23. "To <u>proclaim</u> liberty to the captives, And the opening of the prison to *those who* are bound" (Isaiah 61:1).

Speaking to Things
OLD AND NEW WINESKIN PRAYING

Jesus and the apostles regularly spoke to "things" (the weather, people's bodies, etc.). They declared more than they asked in prayer. As we understand this more and more, it is part of a "new wineskin" of praying.

Old and New Wine Skin Praying

Old	New
Beg	Declare
Pray hard	Pray believing
Many words	Few words
Belief during prayer	Belief after prayer
Reactive	Proactive
Talk about problem	Talk to the problem
Stop devil and curses	Release God and blessing
Focus mainly on problem	Focus on testimonies and promises
Mostly asking	Mostly thanking
God is reluctant or hindered	God is good and has won the victory
Uncomfortable with silence	Values soaking prayer
Worship prepares for prayer	Worship is prayer
Fast to convince God	Fast to transform beliefs
Fasting is an event	Fasting is a lifestyle
Burdened	Joyful
Laughing is rare	Laughing is frequent
Focus on duties of prayer	Seek the depths of God
Expect spiritual attacks	Expect blessings/protection

This list starts with the old attribute of begging and the new wineskin of declaring. There is a time to cry out for mercy and help (Hebrews 4:16), but too often those who beg in prayer are like the disciples in the boat in Mark 4 (mistakenly believing they must rouse a sleeping God).

New mindsets must precede higher levels of prayer. "I will give you the keys of the kingdom of heaven, and whatever you bind on earth will be bound in heaven, and whatever you loose on earth will be loosed in heaven" (Matthew 16:19). When we add this to Matthew 6:10, "Your kingdom come, Your will be done, On earth as *it is* in heaven," we are given a glorious direction that will help our prayer indeed go to these higher levels.

We have been given the keys of the kingdom. Keys represent authority, privilege and the ability to access different realms. Jesus has given us powerful keys, and there is an expectation that we will use them to "bind" and "loose." We bind those things that exist on earth that are not in heaven (discord, sickness, poverty, rebellion, etc.), and we loose what is in heaven but not present on earth (peace, salvation, health, protection, forgiveness, etc.). We will only do this if we believe we have been commissioned to do so. And all of this requires us to speak forth declarations (binding and loosing) that tell circumstances and situations how they are to be.

It may be difficult for us to understand how this is to work, but the Lord will teach us. The journey into higher aspects of prayer will cause a growing sense of dominion in us because we will know that we can make a difference. It also releases joy because of a <u>knowing</u> that things are changing through declarations of binding and loosing (especially loosing because releasing the positive is more powerful than simply trying to stop the negative – darkness must flee when the light is turned on).

This new wineskin of prayer includes a whole lot of speaking to yourself and to things. It makes me think that we may be crazy if we don't talk to ourselves and to the things in our lives.

Speaking to Things
PROPHESY TO THESE BONES

"And He said to me, 'Son of man, can these bones live?' So I answered, 'O Lord GOD, You know.' Again He said to me, '<u>Prophesy to these bones</u>, and <u>say to them</u>, "O dry bones, hear the word of the LORD! Thus says the Lord GOD <u>to these bones</u>: 'Surely I will cause breath to enter into you, and <u>you shall live...</u>'"' So <u>I prophesied as I was commanded</u>; and as I prophesied, there was a noise, and suddenly a rattling; and the bones came together, bone to bone. Indeed, as I looked, the sinews and the flesh came upon them, and the skin covered them over; but *there was* no breath in them. Also He said to me, '<u>Prophesy to the breath</u>, prophesy, son of man, and <u>say to the breath</u>, "Thus says the Lord GOD: 'Come from the four winds, O breath, and breathe on these slain, that they may live.'" So I prophesied as He commanded me, and breath came into them, and they lived, and stood upon their feet, an exceedingly great army" (Ezekiel 37:3-10).

This is a powerful story with truths that will help us bring resurrection life to "dead" or "very dry" (see 37:2) things around us. Ezekiel is asked if the bones can live. God certainly knew the answer, but He wanted to show Ezekiel (and us) the influence that one person can have on situations that look very dead.

Ezekiel was not instructed to pray to God for the bones to come alive, but He was commanded to <u>speak to the bones</u>. The prophet was also told to talk to the breath and the four winds so that life could come. **God apparently chooses not to bring this revival unless He partners with a person who speaks into the situation.** The Lord "needed something to work with" (a declaration) for His will to be done.

Ezekiel had to move from a beggar mentality to a mindset of knowing he had authority in God to powerfully and positively influence circumstances that appeared hopeless. We also are confronted constantly with heavenly questions about whether things can really change. Can this marriage live? Can this city live? Can this generation live? Can this church live? Can this dream live? Can this nation live? Can I really live? **We must move beyond a passive and fatalistic response of "You know, oh Lord" to a place where we are willing to speak directly to these things.**

Let's make this more practical and consider how we could become a greater influence in helping a particular ministry come alive like never before. Here are some "Ezekiel steps" you can take to see a church "live and stand upon its feet to become an exceedingly great army":

1. Pursue revelation on the authority of the believer in Christ. Spend priority time eliminating doubt concerning this. Get mega-doses of teaching that explains the principles that are contained in this book.

2. Speak to your church. Prophesy and say, "You are alive. You are healthy. You walk in abundant power, love and provision. You are being used to propel worldwide revival." You can speak to your church wherever you are, but I suggest that you actually go to your building and speak to it. (Take someone with you for a great experience.)

3. Speak to catalytic forces that will impact your church (i.e. the breath and four winds). Say, "Revivalists, come. Apostles, come. Prophets, come. Leaders, come. Finances, come. Joy, come. Miracles, come. Healing, come."

4. Purpose to not withdraw your faith concerning what you have spoken, but feed your faith through thanksgiving and seeing with your sanctified imagination the things already done in the spirit realm.

You are commissioned to speak to dead circumstances around you and see them come alive. Yes, it may take some getting used to; but as you do, you will begin to notice a sense of empowerment in you and a belief that brings resurrection life all around you. You know what? YOU'RE CRAZY IF YOU <u>DON'T</u> TALK TO YOURSELF and the things in your life.

Speaking to Things
"CRAZY" LIKE JESUS

Here are three different passages about talking to things:

#1 **"Lazarus, come forth!"** Jesus called Lazarus out of the tomb. He had been dead so long (four days) that he "stinketh." It seemed too late, but it wasn't. Jesus said, "If you would believe you would see the glory of God" (John 11:40).

Jesus did not ask His Father to raise Lazarus, but <u>He spoke to the dead body</u>. His words infused Lazarus with life. Jesus is our model of how to bring life to dead places and dead things. ("God, who gives life to the dead and calls those things which do not exist as though they did" – Romans 4:17.)

Lazarus came forth out of the tomb wrapped in grave clothes from head to foot. This must have been a scary sight. It is

79

important to know that the things we call forth may not look pretty at first, but they will as we persevere.

#2 **"Jesus said to [the fig tree], 'Let no one eat fruit from you ever again'"** (Mark 11:14). Later, in Mark 11, it states that the fig tree had dried up from its roots. This is also very instructive for us, as it teaches us that deposits in the spirit realm will eventually affect the natural realm. Those who speak to things must understand that their word of faith immediately starts affecting "roots" in the unseen dimension. Just as the effects of Jesus' words to the fig tree were not immediately seen, the influence of our declaration is generally not visible right away either. This is significant to realize so that we don't withdraw our faith when things don't look like they are changing.

When asked about the fig tree withering away, Jesus said, "I say to you, whoever says to this mountain, 'Be removed and be cast into the sea,' and does not doubt in his heart, but believes that those things he says will be done, he will have whatever he says" (Mark 11:23). Jesus tells us that the fig tree is merely an example of what we are called to do. He states an astounding truth that whoever believes that his words are powerful "will have whatever he says." It would behoove us, as we understand this, to spend much time eliminating the roots of doubt concerning our identity and regarding what we can do through the spoken word. These roots largely come from religious tradition that has shaped our beliefs rather than believing God's Word for what it actually says. One way to combat this unbelief is to pray the apostolic prayers of Ephesians 1:15-19 and 3:14-20 over our lives. For example, pray that you may know "the exceeding greatness of His power toward us who believe" (Ephesians 1:19). Yes, Lord, give us illumination into the power of faith. Take us on a journey to remove all doubt.

#3 **"And the apostles said to the Lord, 'Increase our faith.' So the Lord said, 'If you have faith as a mustard seed, you can say to this mulberry tree, "Be pulled up by the roots and be planted in the sea," and it would obey you'"** (Luke 17:5-6). Jesus said that a little faith goes a long way. Specifically, He tells us that speaking to things with an apparently small amount of faith will accomplish much more than we might think. He also seems to be saying that we will increase our faith by using the faith we have (when He is referring here to the kind of faith that gives decrees to the things in our life). Yes, talking to things is a key to ever increasing faith. Even though it may seem irrational, We're crazy if we <u>don't</u> talk to ourselves and to the situations and things in our lives.

Speaking to Things
A NORMAL DAY OF SPEAKING TO THINGS

Speaking to things should be a big part of the normal Christian life. There are two main reasons for this. First, as Jesus said, "The words that I speak to you are spirit, and *they* are life" (John 6:63). Our decrees impact the spirit realm much more than we realize. They cause a rearranging in the roots of circumstances that will eventually manifest in the natural realm. Secondly, our words cause an increase of faith in our lives. Romans 10:17 says, "Faith comes by hearing." When we speak to a circumstance and then thank God on a regular basis for what is happening (even if we don't see evidence of change), our faith will grow concerning the situation. And our faith level is ultimately the deciding factor concerning whether our life and circumstances are moving forward into God's promises or not.

So what does a life of speaking to things look like? Here is a sample of things spoken on an average day:

1. Steve, come forth today. Arise into your destiny.
2. Home, you are blessed and protected. I deposit peace into you. (See Matthew 10:13.)
3. Son or daughter, you are a lover of Jesus. You're blessed. You make good decisions. You are protected and healthy.
4. Car, you function well and are protected from all accidents.
5. Ralph, I say to your body, be strengthened in Jesus' name. I say to your arm, come into proper alignment. Be healed.
6. Weaverville, I bless you in the name of Jesus. You are in revival. Your schools are blessed. Your government walks

in integrity and wisdom. Your churches are strong. You are prosperous. You fan the fires of worldwide reformation.

7. Mountain of debt; be removed in Jesus' name.

8. Church building, the presence of God is increasing in you. God encounters are released in you like never before.

9. Young people of Trinity County, come forth into your calling as revivalists. Be healed emotionally and relationally.

10. I say to you, Highway 299, you're a safe road. People find Jesus and revival on you because of God's glory.

11. Lewiston, you are a cancer-free zone.

12. New businesses with good paying jobs, come forth.

13. Winds of revival and renewal, blow on our churches. Laborers and backsliders, come forth into your destiny.

14. Ideas and creativity be released in Jesus' name.

15. I loose peace and hope into that situation.

16. Finances, come forth. The Lord is our shepherd. We don't lack.

17. Confusion, be gone in Jesus' name.

18. Lumber mill, you are blessed, safe and prosperous.

These types of declarations are joined with an abundance of verbal thanksgiving for things prayed for or decreed in the past.

Some of you are probably thinking, "It is not right to say these things. It feels like I am commanding God to do something and that can't be right." I used to think that, too. It's true that we need to be grounded in scripture, and we need to be living for the glory of God in order to walk in these truths with integrity, but we cannot disregard a great truth because of a fear of excess.

Finally, it is also important to remember that we will need to persevere through many situations when it seems it is not working or it appears that things are actually getting worse. Again, we don't deny the negative situations (and we need to respond with godly wisdom concerning them), but we must recognize that we are on a journey toward speaking to things without doubting. It may take some time, but the pilgrimage is a wonderful experience of discovering who we are in Christ. Remember, you're crazy if you quit talking to yourself and to the things in your life.

Chapter Seven

Prophesying And Seeding The Clouds Of The Future

PROPHESYING AND SEEDING THE CLOUDS
ESPECIALLY THAT YOU MAY PROPHESY

"Pursue love, and desire spiritual *gifts,* **but especially that you may prophesy**" (1 Corinthians 14:1).

The words "especially that you may prophesy" reveal a great truth for the Christian who wants to make a big impact. The Bible says that this is to be the most sought after spiritual gift. God puts it above eight other powerful gifts that He mentions in 1 Corinthians 12:7-10. Prophecy is to be desired more than the gift of healing, miracles, discerning of spirits, tongues, etc. We understand that all the gifts are to be desired, but prophecy is at the top of the list. Why?

Prophecy is to have the greater focus because prophetic words give God something to work with like nothing else (and ultimately open the door for the other gifts). This becomes especially evident when we understand the New Testament purpose of prophecy. "But he who prophesies speaks edification and exhortation and comfort to men" (I Corinthians 14:3). Edification means to build up. Exhortation is an encouragement to dream higher, to persevere and to realize everyone has a tremendous purpose in God. And comfort makes God's love and promises real even in the toughest of times. Every person needs prophetic people who speak edification, exhortation and comfort. And we all need to especially make sure we become that to others as well.

We are all called into a prophetic ministry. Most of us won't occupy the office of a prophet (see Ephesians 4:11), but we are all called to prophesy. We don't need to have a beard or wear robes to do so. We don't need to use King James language. It is not necessary to say, "Thus saith the Lord . . . " All that we need is love for others, a heart of humility, an understanding of the heart of God and a willingness to step out and speak into lives. New Testament prophesy does not focus on what is wrong with people, but it calls out the gold in them so they can rise in faith to be all that God has destined them to be.

Certainly we need those in the office of a prophet and other leaders who bring correction when needed, but that is not the purpose of prophecy as described in 1 Corinthians 14. With this gift, we are to inspire others, encourage them and reveal God's love. Even though it is a supernatural gift, it is not as mystical as one might think. We can start our prophetic journey by speaking out the positive things we see God doing in others. We can grow in it by sharing impressions with others that we are receiving (highlighted Bible passages, unusual coincidences, mental pictures, etc.). It is amazing what God does as we speak life to others. (As a word of advice, avoid speaking directional changes for lives, correction, negative premonitions or dates for things to happen. And, by all means, stay in good relationship with the leaders of the ministry where you are prophesying.)

Here are some things you can to say to others that are examples of what I am talking about:

"As I was praying this morning, I felt impressed by the Lord to tell you that Philippians 1:6 is for you. God has begun a good work in you, and He will complete it."

"I sense that God is bringing you into a time of deeper intimacy with Him."

"I believe that the Lord wants me to tell you that you are to dream higher for your life. There are gifts inside you that are much bigger than you think."

"Son (or daughter), you have greatness in you. I am so proud of you. God will reveal Himself to you in a powerful way in your life."

"As I think of you, I keep getting the impression that the Lord is preparing you as He prepared David with the sheep. He is doing a mighty thing in you, and you will be a key person in kingdom advancement in the days ahead."

"I feel that I am to tell you that God not only loves you, but He is in love with you."

Prophetic words are so powerful! They are catalytic for others to gain courage, to gain vision and to deepen their relationship with God. Life is in the power of the tongue, and prophesying is part of that life. We're crazy if we don't talk to ourselves and to the things or people in our lives.

PROPHESYING AND SEEDING THE CLOUDS
HELLO, MIGHTY ONE OF VALOR!

"Now the Angel of the LORD came and sat under the terebinth tree... while... Gideon threshed wheat in the winepress, in order to hide *it* from the Midianites. And the Angel of the LORD appeared to him, <u>and said to him</u>, '**The LORD *is* with you, you mighty man of valor!**'" (Judges 6:11, 12).

The story of Gideon in Judges 6 is rich with truth for our Christian walk. The children of Israel were oppressed and in bondage to the Midianites. They were crying out to God for deliverance. In answer to this prayer, God sent an angel to prophetically speak to Gideon about the future and how Gideon would be used to bring a great victory.

"**Gideon said to Him, 'O my lord, if the LORD is with us, why then has all this happened to us?** And where *are* all His miracles which our fathers told us about, saying, "Did not the LORD bring us up from Egypt?" But now the LORD has forsaken us and delivered us into the hands of the Midianites'" (vs. 13).

Gideon thought that the words of the angel were ridiculous and illogical. They did not line up with his experience. How then could they be true?

His response is how most of us feel when we hear a prophetic word for our lives. "Who me?" we say. "You obviously have the wrong person. And besides, if the Lord was with us, things would not be in such a mess." Reactions like this reveal that we don't understand how God brings life to hopeless circumstances and hopeless people. "God, who gives life to the dead and <u>calls those things</u> which do not exist as though they did" (Romans 4:17). In the Old Testament, God often used angels and "big name" prophets to deliver empowering words to people; but in the New Testament, He primarily speaks such things through those who are willing to prophesy to others.

"Then the LORD turned to him and said, '**Go in this might of yours, and you shall save Israel from the hand of the Midianites. Have I not sent you?**'" (vs. 14).

Gideon is prophetically told that he already has the power

(might) to make a difference; and as he "goes," it will manifest into a great victory for all. **He hears the barrier-breaking words** that he "shall save Israel from the hand of the Midianites." This statement is intended to conquer God-limiting lies that Gideon believed and to radically expand his expectation of what the Lord could do through him. We, too, have the opportunity (through prophecy) to break off lies and to ignite people to step forward and "save the people" in remarkable ways.

"So he said to Him, 'O my Lord, how can I save Israel? **Indeed my clan *is* the weakest in Manasseh, and I *am* the least in my father's house**.' And the LORD said to him, 'Surely I will be with you, and you shall defeat the Midianites as one man.'" (vs. 15, 16).

Like Gideon, **it is easy for us to allow our apparent limitations to define who we are and to determine our potential**. Gideon looked at his past to conclude what his future would be. This is a stronghold of thinking that blocks God's purposes and His will. It must be attacked by the spiritual dynamite of prophetic words spoken by those who see beyond constraints in people and beyond their personal histories and ancestry.

How many "Gideons" are in hiding right now waiting for someone to speak to them? They are all around us. They need us to encourage them with life-giving words. Let's open our eyes to others. Let's seek God for a launching word that will birth a revivalist and world changer who will save the people.

Let me say this again: prophetic words are so very powerful! They are catalytic for others to gain courage, to gain vision and to deepen their relationship with God. Remember, LIFE IS IN THE POWER OF THE TONGUE and prophesying to others is part of that life. We're crazy if we don't talk to ourselves and to the things or people in our lives.

PROPHESYING AND SEEDING THE CLOUDS
THE ROMANS 10 GOLD MINE

"For '*whoever calls* on the name of the LORD shall be *saved.*' How then shall they call on Him in whom they have not

believed? And how shall they believe in Him of whom they have not **heard**? And how shall they hear without a **preacher**? And how shall they preach unless they are **sent**? As it is written: *'How beautiful are the feet of those who preach the gospel of peace, who bring **glad tidings** of good things!'* But they have not all obeyed the gospel. For Isaiah says, *'LORD, who has believed our report?'* **So then faith *comes* by hearing, and hearing by the word of God**" (Romans 10:13-17).

This passage in Romans emphasizes the importance of hearing truth in order to be saved. Remember, salvation is much more than going to heaven; but it also includes deliverance, protection, health, victorious living and spiritual power. We need to hear about all that God has done for us through Christ. It is vital that there are people who sense they are sent by God to speak (preach) good news concerning the full benefits of the kingdom.

I once heard that people on the average need to hear the gospel 7.4 times before they believe and become born again. I don't know where this statistic came from (or how accurate it is), but it is clear that most people don't accept the truth about Jesus the first time they hear it. The gospel message needs to gain root in the heart through repetition before the power of eternal life is apprehended. This is not only true about everlasting life, but it is true about every different aspect of our salvation. We must, for instance, hear more than once that we are "more than conquerors" in all areas of life (see Romans 8:37). The need to hear is why prophetic people are so important. They play a critical role in helping people believe the glad tidings about God's plans for their lives.

Just like an evangelist believes in sharing the gospel, we need to have faith that our prophetic words are part of a chain of events that will eventually bear fruit. This must be true even if someone laughs or looks disbelieving concerning the things we say. The truths of Romans 10 help us stay encouraged in this process, but more importantly they propel us to realize:

1. We are **SENT** to prophesy glad tidings of good things.
2. We are called to be a **PREACHER**, which is a messenger

or a herald, (One definition of a herald is fascinating – "<u>somebody who is a forerunner of something or gives an indication of something that is going to happen</u>" – Encarta World English Dictionary).

3. We are to help others really **HEAR** truth so they won't be locked in prisons of bondage and mediocrity. We therefore must commit ourselves to regularly speak forth prophetic words of encouragement, truth and the unfathomable possibilities that are before us in Christ.

4. We become a main reason people **BELIEVE** because we are <u>planting and watering</u> truth regularly. As the hearers believe, they **CALL OUT** to the Lord and experience **SAL-VATION** in the area of this new-found revelation (belief).

Romans 10:13-15 is sandwiched between two great truths that we have studied in this book – "confession is made to salvation" (vs. 10) and "faith comes by hearing" (vs. 17). As we learn to speak to ourselves and to the things in our lives (including people), we look to this portion of scripture as a road map for making a difference in Jesus' name. We'd be crazy if we did not dramatically increase the proactive speaking from our lips as a result.

PROPHESYING AND SEEDING THE CLOUDS
SEEDING THE CLOUDS OF YOUR FUTURE

The Holy Spirit once said to me, "Steve, you often seed the clouds of your future in a negative way and then cry out to me to stop the storm that you have created." God has mercifully answered my prayer many times, but there is a higher way of living.

Imagine with me a cloud over every aspect of your future. It can hover over events coming soon (meetings, ministry opportunities, special occasions or just normal life), or it can be over things years ahead. We have the great opportunity to proactively seed the clouds over these happenings in our lives. Unfortunately, many plant "stormy seeds" and then wonder, "How could God have allowed this to happen to me?"

The spirit of foreboding contributes to this seeding with

substances that will attract difficulty instead of victory. (Foreboding is the confident expectation that bad things are coming.) This apprehension causes many to speak word curses and to have harmful belief systems that sow trouble into the clouds of the days and years ahead. That is a bummer. It is unnecessary, and it needs to stop.

In 2 Corinthians 9 we read, "God loves a cheerful (hilarious) giver." This cheerfulness comes from knowing that generosity will seed the clouds of our future. "But this I say: He who sows sparingly will also reap sparingly, and he who sows bountifully will also reap bountifully... God loves a cheerful giver. And God is able to make <u>all grace abound</u> toward you, that you, <u>always</u> having <u>all sufficiency in all things</u>, may have <u>an abundance for every good work</u>" (2 Corinthians 9:6-8).

Luke 6:37-38 takes this farther. "Judge not, and you shall not be judged. Condemn not, and you shall not be condemned. Forgive, and you will be forgiven. <u>Give, and it will be given to you</u>: good measure, pressed down, shaken together, and running over will be put into your bosom. **For with the same measure that you use, it will be measured back to you**." Incredibly, we can proactively seed our clouds to whatever measure we want, which will bring future "rain" in proportion to our sowing. Now that is something to get cheerful about.

Seeding our future is also powerful in dispelling wrong beliefs (lies) from our lives. A first step in warring against these lies in our thinking is to capture them and replace them with God's promises. Every overcoming Christian has to develop this habit, but it needs to be understood that changing our thinking (repenting) is not just done mentally. It is sped up by getting into the habit of proactively speaking truth and faith into our lives and into our future.

We seed the clouds over our future through our beliefs, our words, our prayers and our actions. Our thoughts (beliefs) primarily will be the cause of spiritual rain or drought. That is why we vigilantly replace thoughts and belief systems that lead to hopelessness, worry and unloving attitudes. Most people, though, find that simply warring in the mind is not enough to uproot old mindsets and to establish new strongholds of hope, joy, love and faith. This is why speaking truth is a key to breaking old mental struggles. **We cannot think a lie when speaking the truth**, and speaking truth ultimately helps create new thoughts and attitudes.

Here is something powerful to do: Take different areas of your future (i.e. ministry, health, finances, family, vocation, protection, evangelism, your nation, your church, miracles, etc.) and spend specific time seeding the cloud over this aspect of life. For instance, choose your vocation and for two minutes say things like: "Thank you, God, that I am blessed in my employment. Thank you that my honesty, creativity, dependability, enthusiasm, and personal blessing create great success for this business and in every business that I will ever be a part of. I will never lack a good job because of how big my God is in me. Jesus has made me successful, and I continually make others successful." Then take additional areas of life and do the same thing. It will ultimately create a "storm" of blessing and godly influence. Wow, we might be crazy if we don't talk to ourselves and to the things in our lives.

PROPHESYING AND SEEDING THE CLOUDS
PUTTING THIS INTO PRACTICE

Let's consider what an average day of talking to yourself (and to the things in your life) looks like.

BEFORE GETTING OUT OF BED:
- ➤ Love on the Lord. Say in your mind, "I love you, Jesus."
- ➤ Replace fear, worry, self-hatred, etc. with thoughts of God's promises.
- ➤ Say as you get of bed, "This is going to be a good day. Thank you, Lord, that your love and promises are true."

AS YOU GET STARTED IN YOUR DAY:
- ➤ Speak truth (scriptural promises or prophetic words) to combat any lie that wants to take your joy or peace away.
- ➤ Speak forth a list of faith declarations.
- ➤ Thank God out loud specifically for things you have prayed for or have been promised in the past.

- ➤ Speak protection and blessing over your life, your loved ones, your church, your city and beyond.
- ➤ Prophesy over your family.

DURING YOUR DAY:
- ➤ Continue to replace lying thoughts with verbal truth.
- ➤ Activate Romans 4:17 and "call those things that are not as though they are." Call your city revived, the young people on fire for the Lord, the churches going to new levels in Christ, the homes healthy and whatever else you are prompted to say.
- ➤ Say, "Thank You" to God for specific things you are believing for.
- ➤ Dispel foreboding and future mediocrity by seeding the clouds of upcoming happenings. When a thought of apprehension occurs, speak forth God's blessing and success into the situation. It is important, though, that you don't just "seed things" that would prevent negative happenings, but determine to be proactive by making affirmations like:
    - There will be many powerful revivalists in my descendents.
    - During the next five years, my influence for Christ will be multiplied greatly.
    - I will write two books a year for the next ten years.
    - I will increase my exercise, nutrition, water intake and laughter in the years ahead.
    - Heroic leaders will be raised up in our country in the next five years.
    - My marital intimacy will be wonderful in my latter years.
    - I will have four strong streams of income in my life that will grow in the next five years.
    - And . . . the list can go on as far as you can believe in the goodness of God.
- ➤ Follow the Joel 3:10 principle ("Let the weak say, 'I am strong'") in whatever area you are falling short of God's

promise. Speak forth who God says you are. For instance, if you are struggling with having spiritual hunger, say, "I am hungry for God." If you're experiencing lack, say, "I have all my needs met according to God's riches in glory." Attack personal weakness with the Joel 3:10 attitude.

➤ Prophesy to as many people as you can. Don't minimize "small" words, words of appreciation or affirmation of good qualities in lives. They are powerfully prophetic in nature. As you grow in confidence and in seeing the gold in people, you can share things like "I am sensing that the Lord wants me to tell you _____."

ENDING YOUR DAY:

➤ Read or speak forth your faith declarations.

➤ Thank God that He is working mightily in every situation that concerns you, and that He is giving you wisdom in everything you are to do concerning these happenings.

➤ Go to bed with worship music or something that will help your heart to be filled with affection for God (and that will help you dwell on His goodness). If you wake in the night with negative emotions, think (or speak if necessary) God's promises related to that area.

Don't be discouraged if you just don't seem to be able to get into a flow in this. Start by making daily declarations and build on that. Just start opening your mouth and intentionally speak more and more. We're crazy if we <u>don't</u> talk to ourselves and to the things in our lives. Truly, life is in the power of the tongue.

PROPHESYING AND SEEDING THE CLOUDS
CHANGING THE WORLD

"**By the blessing of the upright the city is exalted, But it is overthrown by the mouth of the wicked**" (Proverbs 11:11).

I have seen the numbers 11:11 on digital clocks (and in other ways) with amazing frequency in recent years. It has been so repeated that it was obvious God wanted me to seek out its meaning. I sensed in my spirit that Proverbs 11:11 was the answer to this heavenly message. As I read this verse, I was overwhelmed by the truth that I read, and it actually became the reason that I am writing this book.

It is remarkable how we are given assignments from God that we don't ask for. For instance, I have a strong commissioning from the Lord to release joy through my ministry. This is laughable when one considers my stoic background. Also, I have been given the mission to loudly declare that LIFE IS IN THE POWER OF THE TONGUE. My seeing 11:11 continually (it still happens all the time) is my marching order to proclaim this great truth. As Paul told Agrippa, "I was not disobedient to the heavenly vision" (Acts 26:19), we also cannot be disobedient to that which God makes clear to us (even if it does not seem to fit into our preconceived idea of who we are).

Proverbs 11:11 is a mind-boggling Bible verse. It reveals that the future of our cities is in the hands (actually in the mouths) of people who are upright through faith in the blood of Jesus. The blessing of the righteous is much more powerful than the "mouth of the wicked;" but if the saints don't rise up, the ungodly will control the spiritual atmosphere through their word curses by default. This is not God's plan, and He is looking for someone who believes in the power of blessing.

In the Old Testament, there was great faith that a blessing would have tremendous influence for generations to come. This belief is at the root of Proverbs 11:11. The Hebrew meaning for the word "blessing" in this verse means "a benediction; an invocation of good, as of a father about to die." When we verbally bless our cities and regions by faith (and refuse to withdraw our belief), we become a powerful source for God's goodness and salvation to be released. A blessing given by a born-again, spirit-filled person is far superior to any curse invoked from the ungodly. It is also much greater in power than the blessings released under the inferior old covenant (and it was very powerful then). Praise the Lord! I am getting excited thinking about this!

Let's take one step further. It is not just local geographical locations that we can bless, but this verse reveals a principle for other vital areas of life also.

- By the blessing of the upright, the family is exalted.
- By the blessing of the upright, the church is exalted.
- By the blessing of the upright, my finances are exalted.
- By the blessing of the upright, my health is exalted.
- By the blessing of the upright, the future is exalted.
- By the blessing of the upright, the nation is exalted.
- By the blessing of the upright, the neighborhood is exalted.

We can incredibly impact these areas of life by our blessing. As we do, we are prophesying life to them and seeding the clouds of the future. We understand that there are other factors that influence the future wellbeing of these things, but this verse gives us a secret door into a realm of great influence. You know what? Let me say it one final time. **Life is the power of the tongue**. And we are crazy if we <u>don't</u> talk to ourselves and to the things in our lives. May God bless you in the days ahead as you apply the truths of this book.

Three lists of powerful declarations:

A note on these declarations: We won't have something just because we say something, but saying something is necessary to having it. If at the beginning of the 40 days, you don't understand fully why these three sets of declarations are important, then speak them by faith anyway. Some of the first devotionals will give clarity as to their importance.

Declarations #1 The following ten basic declarations are foundational to the building of your faith. They will increase expectancy of God's goodness, and will thus increase the manifestation of that goodness in your life. Say these (and the other declarations lists) every day for a month and see what happens to your life. (Romans 4:17; Romans 10:9,10):

1. My prayers are powerful and effective (2 Corinthians 5:21; James 5:16b).
2. God richly supplies all my needs (Philippians 4:19).
3. I am dead to sin and have a victorious DNA in me (Romans 6:11; Romans 5:17).
4. I walk in ever increasing health (Isaiah 53:3-5; Psalms 103:1-5).
5. I live under a supernatural protection (Psalm 91, Hebrews 8:6).
6. I prosper in all my relationships (Luke 2:52).
7. I consistently bring God encounters to other people (Mark 16:17,18; Acts 3:6).
8. In Jesus, I am 100% loved and worthy to experience all of God's blessings (Colossians 1:12-15).
9. Each of my family members is wonderfully blessed and radically loves Jesus (Acts 16:30,31).
10. I uproariously laugh when I hear a lie from the devil (Psalms 2:2-4).

Declarations #2 Remember this: Faith is the evidence of things not seen (Hebrews 11:1). God's promises, not our circumstances, are our "evidence" for what is really true. We don't deny negative *facts* in our lives, but we choose to focus on the higher reality of God's *truth*. Faith indeed comes by hearing (Romans 10:17); therefore, we choose to speak these powerful truths to build our own faith (believing Romans 12:2 – that our experience will catch up to our beliefs).

1. I set the course of my life with my words (James 3:2-5; Proverbs 18:21).
2. God is on my side; therefore, I declare that I cannot be defeated (Romans 8:37; Psalms 91; Philippians 4:13).
3. I am the head, not the tail. I have insight. I have wisdom. I have ideas and divine strategies. I have authority (Deuteronomy 8:18; 28:13; James 1:5-8; Luke 10:19).
4. My family and those connected to us are protected from disasters, disease, divorce, adultery, poverty, false accusation, foolish decisions and all accidents (Psalm 91).
5. As Abraham did, I speak God's promises over my life so that my faith is strengthened to possess all of God's promises (Romans 4:17-23).
6. I have a sound mind. I think the right thoughts, say the right words, and make the right decisions in every situation I face (2 Timothy 1:7).
7. I expect to have powerful, divine appointments today to heal the sick, raise the dead, prophesy life, lead people to Christ, bring deliverance, release signs and wonders, and bless every place I go (the book of Acts).
8. I expect that today will be the best day of my life spiritually, emotionally, relationally, and financially in Jesus' name (Romans 15:13).

Declarations #3 One of the main "methods" Jesus and the apostles used (in the gospels and Acts) was to SPEAK TO things. You will notice that they did not ask God to heal people, cast out demons, or raise the dead; but they spoke to bodies, demons, the wind, etc. And Jesus, in Mark 11:23, also encourages us to speak to mountains that are in our life.

This set of declarations specifically focuses on our speaking to the various aspects in our lives.

1. My angels are carrying out the Word of God on my behalf (Psalm 103:20).
2. All attacks that were headed my way are diverted right now through angelic protection in Jesus' name (Psalm 91).
3. Just as Jesus spoke to the wind, I say, "Peace be still to my mind, emotions, body and family" (Mark 4:39).
4. I speak to every mountain of discouragement, stress, depression and lack, and say, "Be cast into the sea in Jesus' name" (Mark 11:22-24).
5. I say to this day, "You are blessed!" And I declare that I serve a mighty God, who today will do exceedingly and abundantly beyond all that I can ask or think (Ephesians 3:20). I say you are a good God, and I eagerly anticipate your goodness today.

Made in the USA
Charleston, SC
18 March 2016